Schoolteaching in Canada

DATE DUE

Virtually every Canadian has been influenced, for better or worse, by schoolteachers. Adults recall with clarity experiences with individual teachers; children are in contact with schoolteachers on a daily basis; parents know the importance of teachers in their children's lives. Teachers are the key component in the hotly debated, heavily funded education systems across the country. Theirs is a profession at the centre of often contradictory interests: pedagogic, political, professional, and public.

Alexander Lockhart offers a survey of elementary and secondary schoolteachers and presents a profile of the profession as a whole. Among the topics he discusses are the characteristics of today's teachers, the conditions in which they work, their professional associations, career patterns in teaching, the political environment, current pedagogy, and the public interest.

His findings reflect a profession in transition. In elementary schools two-thirds of teaching staff are women; in secondary schools two-thirds are men. Half of all Canada's teachers are at mid-career, aged 35–49, and near the top of their salary levels. Teachers' salaries have risen faster than the industrial composite in recent years, yet teachers are frustrated in their aspirations. As a group, Lockhart says, teachers have less autonomy than other professionals. Current policy directions and public attitudes aggravate this situation.

Lockhart warns that the teaching profession is moving into crisis. The implications are serious, for our children, and for the quality of life throughout Canada as we look toward the twenty-first century.

ALEXANDER LOCKHART is a member of the Department of Sociology at Trent University.

ALEXANDER LOCKHART

Schoolteaching in Canada

Published in association with Statistics Canada

UNIVERSITY OF TORONTO PRESS
Toronto Buffalo London

University of Toronto Press
Toronto Buffalo London
Printed in Canada

ISBN 0-8020-2748-2 (cloth)
ISBN 0-8020-6788-3 (paper)

Printed on acid-free paper

Canadian Cataloguing in Publication Data

Lockhart, A. (Alexander), 1932–
Schoolteaching in Canada

'Published in association with Statistics Canada.'
Includes bibliographical references.
ISBN 0-8020-2748-2 (bound) ISBN 0-8020-6788-3 (pbk.)

1. Elementary school teachers – Canada. 2. High
school teachers – Canada. 3. Elementary school
teaching – Canada. 4. High school teaching –
Canada. I. Statistics Canada. II. Title.

LB2832.4.L62 1990   371.1'00971   C90-094826-4

For Cameron
May his journey be one of self-discovery and fulfilment.

Contents

Tables

Figures

Preface

This work grows out of a larger seed-bed. In 1984 I was invited to join four other social scientists in a research project on the professions in Canada. This project was initiated and co-ordinated by Dr Paul Reed, Director General, Analytical Studies Branch, Statistics Canada. We were to engage in a broad investigation into the changing circumstances experienced by the particular professional occupation for which each had an established research interest. These professions were: engineering, law, medicine, the professoriate, and schoolteaching. The impetus for the project was the growing recognition that the longstanding relationship between the professions and society was undergoing stress. While a number of finely focused studies of professional occupations existed, there had been little integrative analysis through which a concerned public might acquire insights. Of particular interest was the question of how the social contract between those providing professional services and those in need of those services was being altered by wider social change dynamics.

Of the five occupations chosen for individual study, schoolteaching was the most difficult to fit into a common definition of professionalism. Most positively, schoolteachers meet the fundamental professional criteria of providing a knowledge-based service that holds the promise of improving the lives of its recipients. But despite the extent to which the public has become dependent upon the judgment of teachers, their status as professionals has always been problematical, at least as measured by conventional occupational trait criteria. Yet it is precisely these criteria which have become blurred by the growing number of occupations that have laid claim to professional recognition. Paradoxically, the once seemingly unassailable authority of such quintessential professions as medicine and law is being challenged by a public increasingly concerned about professional integrity and accountability.

Such changes in the relative status of occupations do not occur simply as a consequence of the effort or neglect of those involved. Wider social and economic transformations give rise to changes in the occupational market system as well as in public policy that seeks to regulate that system. This shift in the socio-economic balance inevitably alters the internal organization and external relations of those occupations most directly caught up in the forces of change. Schoolteaching is no exception, and the past three decades have seen some profound changes, as well as some remarkable inertia, in the career system of public school teachers.

This study begins with an overview of the emergence of teaching as a distinctive occupation, and of professionalism as a particular way of delivering personalized knowledge-based services. It then seeks to contextualize the recent changes within the teaching profession by examining statistical trends in terms of a number of analytic variables. These variables are organized within chapters that examine the job market, personal traits, conditions of work, career paths, and collective bargaining patterns of public school teachers. The work concludes with an assessment of the broader private-interest and public-policy issues that emerge from the analysis.

Since this study has been prepared and presented in a way that should makes its insights accessible to an informed, but not necessarily social-science trained reader, a few comments may be in order regarding the process by which factual data at various levels and of various kinds are forged into analytic statements.

First and foremost, it should be understood that holistic analysis of any large institutional domain demands a blending of quantitative and qualitative data sources. As a consequence, the objective statistical measures available in the former are necessarily alloyed in various proportions with the subjective inferences drawn from the latter. The reader needs, therefore, to be aware that theories of social process and action play an important role in guiding the analytic chemistry. While the author feels confident that the conceptual frameworks briefly referenced within this work are appropriate, others may not share the same assumptions. In the final analysis, the determination of 'construct validity' in any such broadly integrative study will depend less on technical criteria than on the reader's own sense of the relevance of the derived insights. It is one of the ironies of social science research that the more one attempts to define the research subject in ways that preclude analytic uncertainty, the more one risks being 'rigorously' irrelevant! If this study does nothing more than produce some insightful uncertainty, it will have been worth the effort.

This notwithstanding, it should be noted that there is always a technical dilemma inherent in trying to integrate data at different levels of aggregation. The problem is known as the 'ecological fallacy' and refers to inferential errors that may occur when shifting the analysis from one level of data aggregation to another level of population aggregation. Because public education in Canada falls under provincial jurisdiction, virtually all the available statistical data are aggregated at the regional level. In an effort not to get bogged down in peripheral discussions over regional variation, this study for the most part integrates the ten separate data sources into a national synthesis. The resulting analysis would be at risk if a large regional deviation from the synthetic mean should prevail. Fortunately, detailed comparison of regional data reveals a surprising uniformity along the critical-variable paths. Also, the residual deviations have tended toward convergence over the period of the trend analysis. This provides some reassurance that the attempt to produce a holistic picture has not resulted in gross distortion. Nevertheless, it should be understood that there are bound to be many negating counter-instances to the central tendencies upon which the integrated analysis is built. Whether these exceptions 'prove the rule' is a moot point. Also debatable is the importance of the still significant diversity which is inevitably understated in the construction of comprehensive pictures.

To put the above cautionary comments into more personally meaningful terms, it is doubtful that any teacher, administrator, student, parent, trustee, or concerned citizen will see a perfect reflection of his or her own unique circumstances in the composite picture that is presented here. However, it is sincerely hoped that such a picture will permit all who care enough to look to acquire insights through which their own experiences can be better understood and assessed.

Acknowledgments

This study could not have been completed without the help and support of others. Statistics Canada must be given full credit for initiating, supporting, and assisting the research as well as making material contributions to the final product. However, only the author can be held accountable for the conceptual orientation, as well as for errors and deficiencies in its presentation. This having been noted, it would be a serious omission if special mention was not made of the intellectual leadership provided by Dr Paul Reed in conceiving and guiding the larger project of which this study is a part.

Other Statistics Canada personnel who contributed their knowledge to the study include Doug Lynd and Garnett Picot. Judy Buehler provided invaluable administrative and liaison assistance. Much gratitude is due to the other academic participants in the project. Marie-André Bertrand (professors), Bernard Blishen (physicians), Jacques Brazeau (engineers), and David Stager (lawyers) each took the time to comment on earlier drafts while pursuing research on their own subject. A very special appreciation must go to Professor Emeritus Oswald Hall of the University of Toronto, one of Canada's most senior and respected occupational sociologists, who served as the project's resident scholar and who ensured that academic standards and peer review conventions were scrupulously observed.

A number of other associates also deserve special attention. My former Trent colleague Dr Glen Filson (now with the Adult Education Department at the University of Guelph) undertook the initial on-line search of the literature – for the most part utilizing the unique resources of the Ontario Institute for Studies in Education. Kathy Brimer undertook the content analysis of the collective agreements that are reviewed in Chapter Five. Erica Van Meurs provided a similar summarization of archival material located in Ottawa. Roger Boe organized special data runs of the Carleton University Canadian Class Structure Project. I am also indebted to the anonymous referees who made a number of important suggestions. Trent University ensured the completion of the project by granting me a sabbatical leave during the conduct of this study. It is also impossible to fully credit the contribution of my wife, Dr Elizabeth Lockhart, with whom virtually every aspect of the study's design and execution was discussed.

Finally, I wish to acknowledge the very special contribution made by my close friend and intellectual confidant, the late J. William Bryant. Bill was a senior colleague who, at the start of my own brief career as a secondary school teacher, welcomed my wife and me to the staff of Chandler Park School in Smithers, BC. More than anyone else, Bill demonstrated how teaching at its best could contribute not only to the growth of individual students but also to the integrity of a whole community. Much of the conceptual orientation of this study is deeply rooted in his example and insights.

SCHOOLTEACHING IN CANADA

1

An Overview of Teaching as a Profession

TEACHERS AND LEARNERS

The human species is unique in the world of nature in that nurture plays such a dominant role in its development. It is the ability to acquire and accumulate knowledge that enables a civilized culture to grow out of humanity's genetic seed-bed.

But if learning is an intrinsic feature of human culture, the pedagogic role, as we have come to understand it today, is not. The circumstances that led to the creation of the modern concept of the 'professional' teacher are clear enough. As the means of knowledge storage and transmission became increasingly symbolic, and as human labour in general became increasingly specialized, the separation of productive and reproductive aspects of knowledge became increasingly accepted.

By the time the industrial revolution had succeeded in dividing the economic realm into private and public jurisdictions, those subjected to the dictates of the market-place were less and less willing to bear the cost of knowledge reproduction as part and parcel of producing goods or providing services. These same transitions replaced the ethic of collective security with the ideology of individual freedom. The resulting social dislocation weakened family and community ties, thus creating the need for a more formal source of cultural transmission. As a consequence, learning became synonymous with schooling and the schoolteacher became someone set apart from those who produced the material and spiritual culture. Thus educating the young evolved into a specialized human service activity with a separate rather than integral relationship to core social and economic processes.

The notion of providing specialized human services is by no means limited to schoolteachers. Lawyers and physicians, for example, also provide knowledge-based services that are once removed from the day-to-day realities which affect, or afflict, their clients' lives. Thus, to the extent that they do provide a specialized service for the benefit of their patrons, teachers are 'professionals' in the most fundamental sense.

This professional mantle has been most unambiguously worn whenever a teacher has responded directly, rather than institutionally, to a student wanting to learn. However, the claim to professional status has been much less secure whenever teachers have served as mediators between the intrinsic needs of their students and the extrinsically determined curricular agendas of institutionalized schooling. Since the modern liberal democratic state functions, albeit at times ineptly, as an agency of public mediation among diverse private interests, the issues that affect the professional status of public school teachers have inevitably reflected wider social conflicts.

Such conflict is not in and of itself a bad thing, provided the public debate it engenders produces understanding through which a workable consensus might be forged. However, a comprehensive understanding of the forces that impinge upon the professional status of teachers has been prevented by a number of factors. Not the least of these have been the changes that currently characterize the relationship between all the professions and the society at large. It seems appropriate, therefore, to preface our review of teaching as a profession with an overview of the professions in general.

THE PROFESSIONS: A REVIEW AND ASSESSMENT

Beginning with the work of Carr-Saunders (1933), the most abundant literature to be found on the professions is located within the sociology of occupations (e.g., Vollmer & Mills 1966; Pavalko 1970). The dominant concern has been with the delineation of the working conditions of 'professionals' and how these conditions systematically differ from the working conditions of other 'occupations' (e.g., Goode 1966). A secondary concern is how these differences may inform, or be informed by, such broader sociological phenomena as social stratifications, social control, social integration, and/or social conflict (e.g. Durkheim 1957; MacIver 1955).

From this comparative perspective emerged a widespread consensus that professionals exhibit occupational traits that are uniquely different from the larger occupational field (Millerson 1964). As a consequence, within this so-called trait model, the professional worker is said to be characterized by 'formal mastery' of a body of esoteric knowledge; a lifelong career 'commitment'; a high level of 'autonomy' that is derived first from the 'voluntary' nature of client relations and second from a wider social recognition of the importance of a 'self-regulating' source of expertise in such socially valuable and vulnerable areas as 'health, justice and education' (Pavalko 1971). Finally, the trait model characterizes true professionalism as endowed with an 'ethical altruism' which is codified by the 'collegial association' as part of its wider functions of self-regulation, recruitment, and socialization (Greenwood 1957).

It has been widely argued by the trait model adherents that professionalism offers a more humanistic alternative to industrial organization of personal services. Whereas the professional model is seen to derive from the pre-industrial guild tradition, the dominant industrial occupational model is seen to function primarily within the authority norms of bureaucratic rationality. In Freidson's (1971) words, the 'authority of imputed expertise rather than the authority of office' is for professionals the trait that separates this privileged occupational minority from the bureaucratically organized majority.

As with all 'ideal-typical' constructs, the trait model focuses upon certain quintessential features rather than central tendencies as a means of identifying differences between, rather than common features among, the subject categories. While this may be useful as a descriptive exercise, it must be recognized that the trait model has limited analytic potential. In particular, there is some difficulty distinguishing between the 'is' and the 'ought' dimensions. For example, in discussion the professional's need for self-regulatory autonomy, the trait literature tends to downplay the monopolistic benefits to the professional while emphasizing the quality of personalized services that allegedly could not be provided to the public under either free-market or bureaucratic-accountability arrangements.

Inevitably, such a congenial interpretation of the reciprocity between the private interests of professionals and the wider public interest was bound to spawn some sceptical response. The more radical critics (e.g., Goffman 1961; Goodman 1964; Illich 1977; Liberman 1970; Szasz 1963, 1974) portray professionalism as a fraudulent conspiracy that promotes the opposite of its professed purpose: the physicians' 'medical model' conditions private acceptance of public ill-health; social service professionals become agents of state control; legal practitioners legitimate injustice; and teachers perform social gatekeeping functions that protect the middle class from the equal opportunity promises made to the disadvantaged.

More moderate critics tend to question the 'typicality' of the relatively few independent professionals who inspire the traits against which all are measured. In so doing they either provide evidence that a good deal of professional activity is undertaken within industrial society's bureaucratic organization (e.g., Evans & Laumann 1983; O. Hall 1946, 1948; Parsons 1939) or seek to rationalize the anomalies experienced by employed professionals (e.g., Kornhauser 1962; Vollmer 1966).

A more institutionally linked basis for understanding the changing character of professionalism was achieved when Johnson (1972) applied a political-economy framework to the assumptions of the trait approach. In rejecting the trait model as an analytically insufficient instrument, Johnson shows how it produces a static abstraction that encourages idealization of, rather than insight into, the real world of professionalism. He finds fault with the trait model: first, because it encourages uncritical acceptance of the legitimating rhetoric of the professional advocacy; second, because it is insensitive to the tensions and accommodations that characterize the interaction between occupational groups and the larger society; and finally, because it fails to distinguish between the various kinds and levels of professionalism that have emerged over time and through which an occupational group may make transitions.

Johnson goes on to note that while those occupations that approximate the ideal-typical profession are getting fewer, those that lay some lesser claim to professional status are increasing. But the trait model provides no means of understanding the counter-dynamics of 'deprofessionalization' (Oppenheimer 1979) and 'professionalization' (Hughes 1960). Answers to the questions raised as a result of these trends come only from investigating how 'the changing distribution of power in society has had important consequences for the manner in which the producers of goods and services have related to their customers and clients' (Johnson 1972:37). Particularly at issue is how such change 'produces tension and uncertainty between producer and consumer' in the context of 'mediating institutions.' As with all mediation, 'power relationships will determine whether uncertainty is reduced at the expense of producer or consumer' (Johnson 1972:41).

Johnson's argument for a more dynamic political-economic framework may also be valuable in linking evidence of changes in professional status to broader social change issues. For example, the professions literature emphasizes that although the exceptionalism of the professions represents something of a challenge to the universalistic ideals, practices, and structures of industrial society, the professions are nevertheless seen by the middle class as the ultimate occupational model (Bledstein 1978). This is not hard to understand, given the economic and social status advantages that typically attend a professional career. The net balance at any given time between professionalization and deprofessionalization trends can therefore be taken as an indicator of whether the fortunes of the occupationally based middle class are on the rise or fall (e.g., Wurthnow & Shrum 1983).

However, as Derber (1983) has pointed out, professionalism has both a technical and an ideological component. It is quite possible for some knowledge workers to avoid 'proletarianization' in the sense that they maintain control of the 'means' of their professional knowledge system, while at the same time being systematically deprofessionalized in terms of any meaningful participation in determining the 'ends' to which their knowledge is applied. Professional engineers have been much exemplified as having suffered this kind of alienation from their once high degree of social responsibility, as the vast majority became employees of large private corporations.

In any event, there can be little doubt that the forces that promoted professionalization of hitherto non-professional occupations were rampant in the two decades following the Second World War. These forces included growth in the knowledge-based service sector, rapid increases in overall societal educational attainments, and the embracing of a technocratically administered 'welfare state' approach to the formulation and implementation of social policy.

Of equal importance are the more recent deprofessionalization trends that have run parallel to the growing public scepticism over the presumption that professionally organized forms of knowledge produce the public benefits claimed by their practitioners. The contemporary scene is also characterized by technical changes that for the first time are invading the very heart of the professional knowledge system. These technological changes not only tend to reshape the professional collegial structure into bureaucratic hierarchies (Freidson 1983) but in many cases also provide direct public access to knowledge formerly available only to professionals.

The past decade has also witnessed the progressive breakdown in professional control over admission and licensing. This has in many instances allowed the supply side of the professional occupation market to outstrip the demand side, which had itself become vulnerably linked to welfare state policies that could not be sustained through periods of fiscal crisis. All this has led not only to professional un- and under-employment, stressing further the state's acquired role as 'employer of last resort' (Armstrong 1977), but to a general weakening of professional self-regulation. For example, such once-taboo behaviour as open competition, advertising of services, public airing of collegial differences, and militant fights over remuneration or jurisdiction has produced gaping breaches in the decorum behind which professional monopoly and privilege were once discreetly screened.

It was during this same turbulent decade that gender inequality issues came to the forefront of public consciousness. This focused attention upon a characteristic of most professions not notably featured within the established trait model, i.e., male dominance based upon an essentially patriarchal ideology – an ideology that even in covert form was no longer socially tolerable (Hearn 1982).

Thus, in a relatively short period of time the social climate shifted from one that prompted the editor of *Daedalus* (Fall 1963) to proclaim optimistically that 'Everywhere in American life, the professions are triumphant,' to one which prompted the pessimistic observation of Donald Schon (1983) that there was a 'crisis of confidence in the professions ... rooted in a growing ... skeptical reassessment of the professions' actual contribution to society's well-being ... In public outcry, in social criticism, and in the complaints of the professionals themselves, the long-standing professional claim to a monopoly of knowledge and social control is challenged – first, because professionals do not live up to values and norms which they espouse, and second, because they are ineffective' (11–13).

While such sentiments regarding professional behaviour are by no means unsupported by evidence, the real source of public disenchantment may be more indicative of a growing scepticism over the ability of technological rationality to provide solutions to those very problems which technical specialists were bound to produce in the first place (e.g., Grant 1969). For if Schon is correct in arguing that the post-modern professional is essentially a 'technician' only capable of pursuing 'predefined problems' in pursuit of 'preestablished goals,' then any attempt to apply such purely instrumental knowledge to essentially moral or political issues is bound ultimately to expose the practitioner as either incompetent or in pursuit of some hidden agenda (King & Malaanson 1972).

While some professional groups and individuals have no doubt resisted this means/ends separation of their specialized 'technical' expertise from a more general 'ideological' understanding of their wider social role – to employ Derber's (1983) useful distinction – there can be little doubt that the pervasive industrial trend toward occupational specialization has penetrated the professions in ways that have inevitably diminished the average practitioner's broader humanistic understandings. So if the public's trust in the ability of professionals to regulate themselves in accordance with the ambient social value consensus is on the decline, then professionals are only partly to blame for their public relations difficulties – for the external forces that seek to neutralize industrial society's few remaining islands of independent judgment are indeed pervasive.

Nowhere in Canada have these external forces been more palpable than in Quebec, where the socio-economic evolution that spanned a century or more in most western societies was dramatically compressed into the decade of the 'quiet revolution.' In an extraordinarily candid account of the very changes in the ambience that Johnson (1972) identified, l'Office des professions du Québec (1976) traces 'the evolution of professionalism in Quebec' from its broad classical education origins, which prepared professionals to 'engage in autonomous and isolated private practice ...' (51), to the contemporary 'conditions of professional employment [that] are characterized ... by a greater number of skilled, salaried people in the labour force, the division of fields of knowledge and Government intervention in supplying essential services' (66).

As a consequence of this 'salarization,' 'fragmentation,' and 'governmental intervention; l'Office argues that the concept of

[specialized occupational] interdependence has replaced that of [professional] autonomy ... More or less directly, the Government is the principal employer of professionals or the principal client for professional services offered in private practice. This significantly changes the relationship between professionals and their clients ... The government can, in fact, pass laws enabling it to directly control a [professional] work activity. It can also pass various laws of a more general nature which regulate more indirectly the distribution of professional services. (52–4)

The policy conclusions that flow from these observations are devastating to the traditional vision of professional autonomy. Of the two categories of professional recognition available under Quebec's Professional Code, it is the externally controlled 'reserve of title' category and not the autonomous 'exclusive right to practice' patent that is seen as appropriate to the needs of the evolving society (65).

The policy statement goes on to identify the sources of professional opposition: 'It is evident to l'Office that professional corporatism will be challenged by private companies as well as by public organizations and institutions ... As a consequence, l'Office intends to recommend, if need be, legislative amendments aimed at allowing the [professional] corporations to assume an effective role in salaried environments, *taking into account the respective jurisdictions of employers and unions*' (67–9, emphasis added).

Few political jurisdictions have been so forthright in providing the reasoning behind official efforts to stem the tide of professionalization – and few have spawned such virulent counter-attacks from those predominantly public-sector knowledge workers who have been forced to adopt unfamiliar proletarian tactics in defence of their professional aspirations (Harp & Betcherman 1980).

Whatever the sources of public disenchantment with 'professionalism' may be, the net effect has been to alter the socio-political ambience from a view which accepts professionalization as a universal good to one that encourages deprofessionalization. Gone, seemingly, is the notion widely promulgated by the early trait literature that professionalism acts as a kind of accessible and humanistic counterforce to the alienating tendencies of complex organizational administration. Gone, too, is the neat trichotomy that placed the 'professional,' the 'bureaucratic' and the 'union' occupational environments into mutually exclusive compartments (Taylor 1968).

Given this, it is not surprising to discover that the once-pervasive interest in studying the professions and their traits declined. For example, a survey of the academic literature between 1976 and 1982 revealed a dramatic reduction in publications devoted to professionalism. This same survey, however, found a reciprocal growth in the study of occupational gender bias, changes in quality of work life, job redesign trends, technological displacement, and white-collar unionization (R.H. Hall 1983).

As if to underscore the point, another long-time observer of the professions, Elliot Freidson, in a 1983 article entitled 'The Reorganization of the Professions by Regulation,' provided a definitive answer to the tentative questions raised in his 1971 anthology *Professions and Their Prospects.* Reviewing the regulatory evidence of the previous decade, Freidson concluded that the professions had in general been subjected to three sources of systematic limitations to their autonomy: 'deregulation' (meaning regulation by the market through the removal of professional monopoly protection), 'mandated peer review' (meaning enforced public audit of professional practices), and 'bureaucratic regulation' (meaning direct accountability to external authority).

As a consequence of these observations, it should be self-evident that any contemporary study of a profession that neglects to 'environmentalize' its analysis within a wider institutional framework runs the risk of failing to capture the critical variables.

TEACHING AS A PROFESSION

At the heart of the traditional concept of the professional organization of work lies the notion of collegial, as distinct from hierarchical, control over the organization and delivery of a knowledge-based service. Only through the maintenance of such autonomy, it is argued, can the privileged relationship between the professional and the client be fostered and maintained. The ideological justification for this relationship focuses upon the professional's responsibility for delivering the service in the *unmediated* best interests of the client. It is further argued that only under such unmediated circumstances can the client have complete trust in the professional's ability to determine, within the boundaries of collegially sanctioned practice, the most appropriate means of meeting the client's needs.

However, before the legitimacy of such an unmediated relationship can be expected to become widely accepted, the client must have the right to seek second opinions and/or to terminate the relationship at any point that dissatisfaction manifests itself. In this sense the client exercises a *passive* form of autonomy as a reciprocal to the professional's active autonomy. Thus, from either the practitioner's or the client's perspective, the essential meaning of 'autonomy' is that no third-party involvement or intervention is tolerated.

But as Johnson (1972) points out, the number of occupations that can still claim this 'collegiate' form of autonomy involving voluntary clients is few, and getting fewer. Even within traditionally self-regulating professions such as medicine and law, various 'mediative' mechanisms are increasingly intervening into the professional/client relationship. This has caused Marcus (1973) to speculate that precisely because public school teachers have always been 'denied full professional status,' they will become 'the prototype of the new and emerging professional' (191). The reason for this prediction is quite simply that the organizational conditions under which teachers typically work, i.e., 'bureaucratization, large size, external intervention, specialization among members, and societal demands for accountability even with the absence of performance criteria' (191), are now impinging upon the medical, legal, and academic professions.

Whether prototypical or not, there can be little doubt that public school teachers in Canada have never enjoyed anything approaching collegiate autonomy. In summarizing the extensive evidence on the conditions of work of schoolteachers, Corwin (1965) offers the following assessment: 'Teachers have virtually no control over their standards of work. They have little control over the subjects to be taught; the material to be used; the criteria for deciding who would be admitted, retained, and graduated from training schools; the qualifications for teacher training; the forms to be used in reporting student progress; school boundary lines and the criteria for permitting students to attend; and other matters that affect teaching' (246).

Henchey (1977) goes even further in delineating the manifold sources of restriction on teacher professionalization:

In many ways teaching has always been a derived – profession. For its moral authority it has looked to church or government; its intellectual criteria have been traditionally found in the field of psychology and in the various academic disciplines which teachers are expected to serve; its value has been measured in the currency of sociology and economics. Teachers ... have always worked within a structure that was essentially paternalistic and one in which the *pater* usually belongs to some other profession. [As a consequence] ... teachers, despite their growing influence, were unable to construct a pattern of professional autonomy ... The most decisive factor ... was the speed with which the system was industrialized in a hierarchical structure with the minister of education at the top, followed by layers of department officials, regional offices, school board administrators, consultants, school administrators, non-teaching professionals, and – classroom teachers at the bottom. (147–9)

Indeed, the legally defined rights and obligations of public school teachers in Canada, while demonstrating some regional variation, have historically placed rather uniform decision-making constraints upon teachers. For example, in his exhaustive documentation of Ontario's public education system, Fleming (1971: 423ff) delves into the professional autonomy implications of that province's (then) School Administration Act (1970). He notes, for example, Section 22, which requires the teacher to 'teach diligently and faithfully the subjects in the course of study as prescribed by the regulations ... to maintain proper order and discipline in his classroom and while on duty in the school and on the playground under the direction of the principal; ... to see that the classroom is ready for the reception of pupils at least fifteen minutes before the time of opening in the morning and five minutes before the time of opening in the afternoon' (425, 426).

Section 49 forbids teachers to run for election to school-board office in their own districts. Fleming notes that while the government looked favourably upon a commissioned report recommending the removal of similar restrictions on municipal employees running for municipal office, they specifically rejected these recommendations for teachers with respect to school-board office. The concern expressed was that teachers who were involved in education policy decisions that might affect their own work would be in a 'conflict of interest' position.

As curious as the above reasoning appears, it highlights what has been in North American public education something of a sacred cow and illustrates what Selby (1977) calls 'the myth of local control.' Despite the systematic increase in centralized control (to be documented in Chapter Five), the veneer of town-hall democracy, in the form of locally elected boards of school trustees, has been carefully preserved.

The negative consequences of this 'local control' ideology upon schoolteachers' professional autonomy have been described by Baron and Tropp (1961) in a comparison of the level of professionalization of English and North American teachers:

whereas in England it is the teacher who represents to the community in which he works 'nationally' accepted values, in America it is the community that interprets to the teacher the task he is to perform. This difference is of supreme importance, because if it can be accepted it explains fundamental differences in the behavior of teachers as a professional body in each country. It explains, at least in England, why the content of what is taught in the schools is virtually never discussed save in professional gatherings of educators, whereas in America constant efforts are made ... to insure that what is done in the schools is done with the 'authority' of lay opinion. (546)

If the English comparison is prejudicial to the Canadian situation, Stabler's (1979) comparison of the level of 'self-government' enjoyed by Canadian and Scottish teachers is utterly devastating. In the case of Scotland, the autonomy of teachers approaches that of the traditional, independent practitioner professions. It 'include[s] the right of the profession to control admission by setting qualifications of education and competence, to determine and maintain a code of ethics and conduct, and to take disciplinary action against a member who fails to meet these standards' (1). Yet despite the North American tradition that teachers defer their professional knowledge claims to local lay wisdom, the competence of local boards has been questioned. For example, Holdaway's (1970) content analysis of topics discussed at Alberta school-board meetings revealed that the largest single agenda item related to the physical plant, while only 10 per cent of the items concerned school/community relations. Student-related items occupied only 7 per cent of the board's interest, and curricular matters just 3 per cent.

Thus, with respect to those functions that are most clearly a matter of professional judgment, local school-boards do not appear anxious to intervene. This conclusion is further supported by Cooper's (1966) study of the employer/employee relations between Alberta boards and their teachers. While local trustees were found to be in essential agreement with their teachers on 'educational issues,' their disagreements focused on working conditions, academic freedom, and related matters. In other words, locally elected trustees, positioned as they are between the professional expertise of their teachers and the bureaucratic power of the central ministry, appear unwilling to get involved in either professional or policy matters.

Given the trend toward amalgamation of local boards into regional conglomerates, it is also difficult to take very seriously the argument that it is through school-board input that particular community interests are given effective voice. For example, between 1964 and 1969, the Ontario Ministry of Education reduced its 2,544 local boards to 76 (Selby 1977). This effectively eliminated 97 per cent of the locally elected trustees through which community interests might be effectively communicated to the schools. As Lasley and Galloway (1983) note, the sense of community alienation that resulted from this reduction in local control potential did little for the image of teachers as client-centred professionals.

But if there are few mechanisms through which local-level needs and irritants can be communicated directly to teachers, there appear to be even fewer means by which teachers can communicate their professional problems to either the local boards or the central bureaucracy. Baron and Tropp's (1961) comparison of English and North American teacher career systems once again provides insight into this source of isolation. They note that in the English system the headmaster (principal) is organizationally identified as 'first among equals' *within* the teaching staff. In the North American model, the principal is seen as primarily ensuring that the *external* bureaucracy's imperatives are adhered to by the teaching staff. It is then argued that the English model better ensures that the school's chief administrator will identify primarily with the professional needs of the school staff and thus reflect their interests when dealing with outside parties.

This last point hints at yet another source of limitation on professional goal realization. At issue here is the organizational environment which elevates administrative roles over professional roles on the career ladder. Whereas a professionally dominated career system assumes that career success is measured and rewarded *within* the realm of professional competence and practice, a bureaucratically dominated career system may make the mistake of adopting success and reward criteria that focus attention on moving into the administrative hierarchies that lie *outside* the realm of professional practice and recognition. This distinction is perhaps best illustrated by considering the academic career system of university professors. Like schoolteachers, professors are employed within complex bureaucratic organizations. But unlike the public school's career system, a professorial career is primarily oriented to professional criteria of success and professional adjudication of rewards. Those professors who take on administrative roles rarely completely abandon their professional duties. When, as is common, they return to full-time professorial duties after serving an administrative stint, professors have no sense of being diminished. Indeed, within this clearly professional career system a too early or too prolonged involvement in administration may reduce rewards, even give rise to peer doubts over professional competence or commitment. In the case of the teaching career system, however, the reverse assumption prevails, i.e., failure to achieve administrative rank by mid-career (especially for males) gives rise to presumptions, even among teachers themselves, of career stagnation. Given this, the question must be asked: to what extent does a career system that so obviously values promotion into administrative hierarchies also condition teachers into undervaluing their professional practice commitments?

R.H. Hall (1960) provides a partial answer in a study that compares idealized commitments to professional norms with the actual presence of these traits in the work settings of a number of occupations including teaching. What Hall discovered was an inverse relationship between the idealized commitment to professionalism and the extent to which there were real opportunities for its practice (see also Lipset & Schwartz 1966; Palmatier 1969).

Lam's (1982) application of Hall's model found that it was the low realization of professional working conditions that caused Canadian teachers to exhibit such high levels of commitment to the ideology of professionalism. This study further reveals that teachers lack one important professional trait – they failed to demonstrate the same high level of commitment to their work as a lifelong calling that typifies most other professional groups.

In his Ontario teacher studies, Fris (1972, 1976) discovered that teachers experience a 'frustration dissonance' as a consequence of the gap between their professional aspirations and on-the-job realization. This dissonance is most often resolved through passive resignation or active pursuit of the administrative promotion. While this adjustment behaviour may well reflect a realistic assessment of how to survive or prosper within the career system, it obviously does little to promote professional values and practice.

Yet despite this low level of professional realization, the evidence suggests that public school teachers remain strongly committed to the attainment of greater professional control over their work. In their efforts to gain more control they have encountered strong bureaucratic resistance and in turn have developed tactics aimed at achieving their several but not always consistent professional objectives. While these tactics have unquestionably advanced the material interests of teachers, they have done little to reduce public confusion, even cynicism, with respect to the intrinsically professional issues of educational quality and accountability.

The speed with which the public educational system shifted from frantic expansion to controlled contraction has also affected the professional opportunities and priorities of teachers as well as their relationship with employers and the public. The resulting preoccupation with fiscal constraint has done little to help focus attention on how the sometimes separate, sometimes common, interests of teachers, educational administrators, parents, and the community should be addressed politically.

It is apparent that the occupation of schoolteaching is undergoing a crisis that threatens the integrity of one of the most all-encompassing public service institutions in the nation. If this crisis is to be effectively resolved, some greater awareness of the realities, as distinct from the ideologies and mythologies, of the occupation of schoolteaching is required of all concerned.

The chapters that follow seek to provide, within the limits of available data, a comprehensive picture of the social characteristics and institutional dynamics that together define the occupational realities of Canadian schoolteachers. In interpreting the various data bases from which the analysis is drawn, three analytic features are emphasized: 1) the demographic and economic changes that have occurred over the period following the Second World War to the near present; 2) the organizational dimensions within which the recruitment, training, practice, and rewarding of public school teachers takes place; 3) how both of these dimensions have affected teachers relative to other occupational groups. Although it is not the purpose of this study to provide ameliorative prescriptions, the concluding chapter places the analysis within a broader framework, which may help the variously affected constituencies to identify some potentially useful bases for communication and action.

2

The Market for Schoolteachers

Canada conforms to the basic public educational norms that obtain in most modern societies, that is, the state provides a dozen or so years of free, universal, and (to the age of sixteen) compulsory schooling. Based on these norms, the demand side of the teacher labour-market is primarily demographically driven. In essence, the compulsory school-aged population at any moment will, given a set student/teacher ratio, determine the number of teachers required.

Beyond the compulsory grades, the demand for teachers becomes somewhat more elastic, as demographic and institutional factors are less rigidly predetermined. Obviously, the size of the relevant-age population sets the upper limit, while the 'retention rate' – those who continue beyond legal school-leaving age – will determine the actual demand.

On the supply side, the teacher-market is affected by several factors: the overall size of the job-entry population; the education profile of that population in relation to the teacher-qualification requirements; the relative attractions of a teaching career in comparison with alternative careers; the number of years qualified teachers on average teach; and the reserve of qualified but currently inactive teachers.

When all of these labour-market variables are taken into account, the demand side of the public school teacher-market may be described as exceptionally resistant to policy-based adjustments through the basic education levels because of the fundamental rigidity of both the demographic and institutional factors. However, there is some demand-side elasticity at the voluntary age-level in the sense that the marginal consumer's propensity to utilize the service (or the school's willingness to provide service to marginal beneficiaries) may be influenced by educational policy and/or wider institutional factors. For example, after a dramatic rise in the high-school retention rate in the 1960s, the 1980s have seen a major decline.

On the supply side, the teacher-market has a relatively high potential for institutional adjustment. For example, minimum educational requisites, licensing criteria, training accessibility, and the salary and working conditions of teachers are all vested within, or are directly influenced by, either policy or administrative decisions.

We will examine more closely the effect of both public policy and internal administrative practices upon teaching as an occupation in a later chapter. In this chapter the focus is on the less controllable demographic and institutional factors which are likely to continue to determine the market for teachers.

DEMOGRAPHY: THE BATTLE OF THE BULGE

For Canadians, the most salient demographic fact of the twentieth century is the extraordinary deviation from the normal age-distribution profile of the nation's population. Participation in two world wars, boom-bust economic cycles, immigration, and changes in social values all combined to alter dramatically the normal pyramidal pattern of age distribution (Romaniuc 1984; Veevers 1983).

Within the living population, the most significant departure from the normal age composition was caused by the 'baby boom' that immediately followed the Second World War. Coming as it did on the heels of the Great Depression, which produced a historically low fertility rate of 2.6 children per family in 1937, the two post-war decades saw a fertility explosion which peaked in 1959 at a rate of 3.9 children per family. However, by the mid-1970s the rate had dropped to the unprecedented low of 1.8, only to be further diminished to 1.6 by the mid-1980s (SC 11-402, 91-518, 91-520).

The net outcome of this wild fluctuation in fecundity was the creation of a cohort bulge that would move through the social and economic structure like a tidal wave. In terms of the demand-side effects on age-specific service institutions, this wave would produce a massive inflation, followed by as dramatic a deflation, in employment opportunities. Figure 2.1, which reproduces the age-stratified profile of the Canadian population for 1971 and (superimposed) 1982, provides some indication of the progress of this age distortion.

Inevitably, the school system would be among the first of these age-specific institutions to be affected. The population 'bulge' was therefore bound to increase the demand for schoolteachers in the compulsory attendance grades in direct proportion to the school-age population expansion. However, this same post-war period was also characterized by new economic theories and public policies which promoted the belief in education as a panacea for social and economic ills. This, in turn, had the effect of increasing the non-compulsory age retention rates, which grew from 53.5 per cent in 1955 to a peak of 87.9 per cent in 1970 (SC 81-569).

It is noteworthy that the secondary source of enrolment variability, the participation rate, paralleled the increase and then decreased in the major demographic factor. In fact, as Figure 2.2 reveals, the actual school enrolment briefly exceeded the official school-age population statistic just prior to the enrolment peak in 1970. The apparent impossibility of having greater than 100 per cent participation is explained by the fact that the official school-age population had been for some time established as the age 6 to 17 population whereas by 1970 the school-age range had been extended to include many 5-year-olds at the primary level and those age 18 to 19 at the secondary level. These statistical anomalies notwithstanding, it is apparent that as the proportion of youths in the population increased, so too did their propensity to remain longer in school. However, the converse has also obtained. As the school-age sector of the population proportionally declined, their propensity to remain in school to normal completion has also declined.

As a consequence of these demographic and institutional factors, the number of full-time elementary and secondary teachers in Canada more than doubled between 1955 and 1970. As Table 2.1 reveals, while school enrolments were increasing by two-and-one-third times the total population growth, the teaching force actually expanded by three-and-one-half times over the same period. Thus, the supply of teachers not only kept pace with, but exceeded, the growth in student numbers during the expansionary period. It would seem that in reacting to the uncontrollable population pressure, no one considered the possibility of invoking the more controllable institutional factors in a counter-cyclical way. On the contrary, as will be discussed in another context, what discretionary policy instruments were available to the system's planners and administrators were overwhelmingly exercised in a direction that only further exacerbated the demographically driven supply/demand imbalances. For example, the student/teacher ratio fell from a nominal 26.6 in 1955 to a nominal 18.5 by 1980, with the major shift paralleling the period of rapid enrolment declined (Table 2.1). Figure 2.3 compares student enrolments with teacher employment before and after the 1970 shift from increasing to decreasing enrolments.

It is also noteworthy that the same optimistic public policies and popular ideologies had also dramatically increased the post-secondary participation rate. The initial effect of this longer educational retention was to reduce the flow of new entrants into the labourforce. But as the baby-boom bulge began to spill over the higher educational dikes, the highly qualified labour-market shifted rapidly from under- to over-supply (Clark & Zsigmond 1981). One of the most ironic features of the massive increase in the number of university graduates that paralleled the school expansion period was that by 1969 over 50 per cent of all university graduates who were working two years after graduation were employed in the public education sector (Picot 1983: Chart 7, Table 8). Thus, for a time, the public education system became a major consumer of is own products – a form of institutional nepotism that could hardly be expected to last.

But as surely as the leading edge of the baby boom increased the demand for teachers, its trailing edge was bound to shift the teacher-market in the opposite direction. By the time the reality of declining enrolments forced some serious effort at teacher-demand forecasting, other population anomalies began to plague the system. For example, through the 1960s demographers had forecast that a second baby boom would quickly follow as the original boomers reached prime fertility age. However, this much-predicted 'echo effect' did not materialize, as a consequence of dramatic shifts in the social and economic ambience that in only a few short years cut fertility rates down to less than half. Indeed, by 1978 one of the more authoritative of the many studies commissioned on the 'challenge of declining school enrollments' (Jackson 1978) warned that future educational planning should be based on a relatively steady-state fertility rate of 1.6 – well below replacement level. Given that Canada was experiencing a fertility rate of over twice that of only twenty-five years earlier, such a forecast seemed rash indeed. Yet by the mid-1980s, the rate had already fallen to this figure.

In Romianiuc's (1984) well-documented and carefully reasoned demographic analysis, three population forecast scenarios to the year 2050 are projected. The low (sub-replacement level) is based upon a fertility-rate assumption of 1.5; the middle (replacement level) assumes 2.1; and the high (modest growth) assumes 2.5. Romianiuc notes that initially there will continue to be some 'population momentum,' i.e., that because of their large numbers, the baby-boom cohort would still produce enough babies (though at later maternal ages) to produce a marginal school-age population increase over the 1970s low. However, once the baby-boomers move out of the reproductive age range, it would take a very significant increase in fertility rates to produce any prolonged aggregate-demand increase in the teacher-market.

Such aggregate-demand forecasts do not, of course, take into account regional and local variations in fertility or migration patterns. Some ethnic minorities, such as Canada's predominantly rural native population, continue to maintain a high fertility rate. Alternatively, the inner-city districts of major economic 'growth pole' centres attract a disproportionate number of low-skill, high-fertility, younger-aged migrants and immigrants, while the city's 'empty nest' retirement cohorts make room by migrating to the de-industrializing peripheral communities. As a consequence, local teacher shortages and surpluses may develop, often on short notice.

The net effect of these demographic anomalies will be to de-stabilize an already unstable teacher-market over both the short and long term. To make matters worse, the public-policy pendulum, which swung in the direction of support for all things educational during the expansionary 1960s, appears now to be swinging in the opposite direction (Cistone 1972; Wilson 1977). Official studies of educational productivity purport to demonstrate that the lowering of teacher-student ratios has not produced measurable improvements in student performance (Educational Research Services, Inc. 1978; Pidgeon 1974; Ryan & Greenfield 1975). Other widely accepted evidence suggests that high retention rates do little beyond lowering overall standards to the alleged detriment of students with higher potential. The rapid rise in the drop-out rate that occurred in the 1980s also suggests that the least advantaged of the nation's youth discovered for themselves what sceptical labour-market analysts (Lockhart 1975, 1977; Paci 1977) have been saying for some time, that the increased school retention (and post-secondary participation) rates that occurred during the 1960s and 1970s did not produce the economic benefits or occupational opportunities that the human capital theory had promised. While the more socially advantaged continue to see advanced education as the necessary, if no longer sufficient, condition for occupational success, many who might otherwise make an earlier departure appear to delay the termination of their schooling because of the manifest lack of entry-level jobs. But if the public education system has acquired, at least in part, the function of providing a socially acceptable alternative to a further increase in youth unemployment statistics, teachers cannot reasonably expect any more padding of their own job-market situation through the lowering of student-teacher ratios.

As a consequence, public policy in the 1980s became characterized by increasingly severe fiscal constraint upon, along with restrictive access to, public education programs. While surveys (e.g., Livingston 1979) suggest that public opinion remains somewhat more loyal to an open-door public education system than do those currently controlling educational spending, the general drift toward 'accountability' and 'productivity' in the public service sector is likely to act as an inhibitor to any further manipulation of the teacher-market in the direction of increasing demand.

THE SOCIAL CHARACTERISTICS OF MARGINALIZED TEACHERS

As noted above, the reduction in the student-teacher ratio was the principal labour-market adjustment mechanism through which massive teacher lay-offs were avoided as the demand for teachers fell rapidly in the 1980s. However, the corollary of this strategy was the emergence of the 'silent firing' syndrome.

Silent firing refers to closing off, or downgrading to temporary or part-time, jobs for new-entrants in order to reserve the maximum benefits for the established work-force. If the 1960s were characterized by a massive expansion in teacher-training capability, the late 1970s and early 1980s were witness to bloated faculties of education disgorging their graduates into an essentially closed market. Efforts to sell the value of teacher education as an appropriate preparation for a variety of non-teaching roles such as public relations and advertising did little to convince either alternative employers or discouraged graduates. As a consequence, recently licensed teachers had to find alternative employment or face prolonged periods of marginality as part-time teachers – a category whose numbers tripled after 1970.

As is common in most occupational surplus situations, the austerity axe did not fall evenly. Insights into who bore the brunt of the low-demand market are revealed in a series of studies that emerged in the era of declining enrolments. Warren's (1979) study of the characteristics of unemployed teachers found the majority to be women, disproportionately young, and from cities with populations over ten thousand. However, 87 per cent did have prior full-time teaching experience (over half with more than five years). Thirty-one per cent of these previously employed teachers (all women) said they left teaching originally to raise a family, while 18 per cent left, most ironically, to upgrade their professional qualifications. Some 27 per cent of the men, but only 5 per cent of the women, said they would be willing to move anywhere within the province for teaching employment.

These same social characteristics reappear in Fagan and Clark's (1979) comparison of the traits of successful and unsuccessful job-seekers among recent teacher-education graduates. The study found that the job-acquisition rate in a surplus market was significantly better for those who were sponsored by established family, friends, or clergy; had incumbent teachers in their immediate family; specialized in French, physical education, or special education; were certified within the primary division; were married males; or came from small communities and were willing to relocate.

While some of these 'successful' characteristics obviously reflect residual islands of demand in a rising tide of over-supply, the 'unsuccessful' traits revealed in these and other studies (see Corman 1979) reflect the characteristic social base of industrial-worker marginality. Specifically, it is women, new-entrants, those without influential sponsors, and those whose mobility is restricted by family obligations or community ties who are forced into reserve-army status. Thus, teaching joined the increasing number of occupations that responded to a surplus market by creating a two-tier membership structure, where security was reserved for the occupationally and socially established while all others were exposed to the dictates of the market-place (Butterick 1977).

Similar social selection biases also became apparent as the supply-side adjustment mechanisms associated with recruitment and licensing began to respond (albeit rather belatedly) to the reversal in the teacher-market. In particular, the abrupt increase in teacher-training entry standards resulted in a significant upward shift in the social class origins of male candidates especially. As will be detailed later, this had the effect of significantly undermining the profession's historic role as an avenue of upward social mobility.

These are the most obvious, but not necessarily the only, factors affecting the teacher-market as it attempts to adjust to the extraordinary pressures that wider socio-economic forces precipitated. Subsequent analysis will seek answers to the question of how the current and likely future adjustments within the teacher-market may affect teaching as an occupation, and public education as an institution.

3

Teacher Characteristics

OVERVIEW

That individuals differ widely in their personal characteristics is hardly questionable. Similarly, social aggregations, from whole nations to nuclear families, may also exhibit quite unique characteristics as a kind of collective property. It is, of course, important to avoid stereotyping individual members of such groups since divergence from the norm is often considerable. However, it is fundamental to occupational analysis to examine to what extent the characteristics of a particular work-force cluster around specific modalities that are over- or under-representative of the larger society.

The properties associated with a given occupation may reflect not only the actual work requirements, but also the social factors: the norms, values, and prejudices of society as a whole, or of those institutions which perform occupational gatekeeping functions. Also, any unique characteristics of an occupation's established work-force inevitably tend to reproduce themselves through the self-selecting process by which potential recruits are attracted to or repelled by the image of occupational role models.

Further, to the extent that occupational hierarchies are themselves a major component in the wider system of socio-economic allocation, it obviously matters a great deal to the collective power base of any given occupation just how the social-status characteristics of the incumbent work-force are predominantly derived and popularly perceived.

Finally, the public image of those who perform crucial public service roles may become as important as their skills in achieving, or failing to achieve, client confidence. This is the case particularly if patrons have few or no alternatives. Under such circumstances, the public sense of security or vulnerability can be strongly influenced by the personal and organizational integrity that characterizes the occupation and its institutional environment.

In this chapter we shall seek, on the basis of available data, an understanding of the collective characteristics of contemporary Canadian schoolteachers. The relevant variables to be examined include: gender distribution, socio-economic and ethnic origins, age structure, educational attainments, and normative patterns as these relate to occupational motivation and practice.

GENDER DISTRIBUTION

Within the general 'professional and managerial' occupational category, teaching is exceptional in that women have historically outnumbered their male colleagues. Teaching is also uncharacteristic in that, for many years now, female teachers have enjoyed equal pay for equal work.

However, if the overall gender ratio is distributed by teaching level and especially between teaching and school administration, it is immediately apparent that men are over-represented at the higher income levels.

Danlewycz, Light, and Prentice (1983) have examined in some detail the origins of the sexual division of teaching labour in nineteenth-century Ontario and Quebec. The major contributors to the traditional predominance of females in the teacher labour-force were found to be the tendency for girls to remain in school longer than their agriculturally oriented brothers, and social pressures that discouraged males from pursuing nurturing roles. Other factors included the (then) low pay and the patriarchal attitudes of the public school authorities (Hoffman 1981; Prentice 1978; Shack 1973; Ward 1974).

While the situation of low pay and restrictive community attitudes which afflicted the early school 'marms' has unquestionably improved in recent years, the question of parallel improvements in overcoming the occupation's patriarchal tradition needs to be looked at closely in the context of the demographic changes already discussed.

The historic data on gender ratio reveals only slight change in the proportion of females in the teacher labour-force, from 77 per cent at the turn of the century to 70 per cent at the beginning of the baby-boom expansion in 1955 (SC 81-568). But, as Table 3.1 reveals, from then on the gender ratio drops rapidly to a meagre 54 per cent female advantage by 1983 (SC 81-202). In terms of the historic observations of Danylewycz et al, this period of educational expansion was one in which the school retention rate differential between boys and girls was narrowing, thus making more males educationally eligible to become teachers. Teacher remuneration also increased, which presumably rendered teaching more attractive to male 'heads of households.'

However, as noted in Chapter Two, this was also a period which produced a major increase in the secondary-level retention rates. The better balance that resulted between the 'nurturing' elementary level and the 'post-nurturing' secondary level offers an opportunity to test the social attitudes which Danylewycz et al identified as historically favouring women in the teaching role. At issue is whether the influx of males into teaching during the massive enrolment expansion period between 1955 and 1970 (Table 2.1) was evenly distributed through all grades or tended to predominate at the secondary level. The answer is clearly the latter. By the peak of the enrolment expansion in 1970, despite a narrowing of the gap between elementary and secondary pay scales, the number of males in elementary teaching had increased by only 1.6 per cent to 28.6 per cent, or only slightly more than one male for every four females. However, at the even more rapidly expanding secondary level, male teachers continued to maintain their historic three-to-one majority (SC 81-568, 81-569, 81-202).

It is interesting to note that although most of the Canadian teacher characteristics discussed here are closely parallel to those in the United States, this congruity does not apply to the secondary-level gender ratio. While the U.S. elementary schools remain, as in Canada, heavily dominated by women teachers (5:1 ratio), the U.S. secondary school ratio is now approaching parity, with men holding only a diminishing advantage at 53.6 per cent by 1982/3 (Feistritzer 1983:27).

In Canada, then, the expansion in the secondary school teacher-demand proved to be much more focused upon male than female recruitment. Given that the secondary school enrolment expansion reflected not only an increasing high-school-age cohort but also a higher retention rate, it would appear that this double source of expansion created employment opportunities primarily for males. Indeed, as Table 3.2 shows, if we compare the change in the proportion of male teachers to the change in the proportion of students who attended secondary schools over the period of rapid enrolment growth, it is apparent that the increase in the enrolments beyond the compulsory elementary levels explains virtually all the increase in the male proportion within the overall teacher labour-force (coefficient of determination = .98).

Recalling the earlier discussion on market variables, it is now apparent that the teacher-market in Canada is strongly gender-segmented. Any differentials that develop between elementary and secondary levels within the overall demand for teachers will therefore have differential gender effects on the supply side. For example, should institutional factors shift in a direction that discourages the high secondary-level retention rates that developed during the 1970s (a counter-trend which actually began in the 1980s), the traditional male-dominant segment of the market would be the most negatively affected. However, it will be interesting to observe how such secondary-level declines, along with changing social attitudes regarding gender roles, may affect male interest in elementary teaching (see Chapter Five).

The question of whether the historic practice of preserving administration positions for males has continued into the present may be similarly examined. At the peak of the enrolment inflows, while the proportion of all teachers who were women was 62 per cent, the proportion who became principals was only 16.9 per cent, and a similar proportion of women, 16.8 per cent, held the office of vice-principal. By 1979/80, when the overall female-teacher proportion had declined to 56 per cent, the proportion of female principals had dropped to 13.3 per cent and the proportion of female vice-principals was down to 15.7 per cent. Even in the elementary schools, where female teachers outnumber male teachers four-to-one, the proportion of women principals was only 19.7 per cent at the enrolment peak, and then dropped to 15.1 per cent by 1979/80.

Female elementary school vice-principals fared slightly better at 20.2 per cent at the peak enrolment period, marginally increasing to 20.4 per cent by 1979/80 (see Figure 3.1).

Thus, close examination of the gender distribution within the hierarchical structure of the public education career system reveals not only a retention of 'traditional' patriarchal social attitudes with respect to who 'nurtures' and who 'commands' but also, as one federal government affirmative action report underscores (Statistics Canada 1980), a strong resistance to the now widely accepted public and private sector equal opportunity promotion policies.

There are, however, two intervening variables that need to be examined in relation to the above conclusions. The first relates to any differences in the relative occupational 'attachment' which males and females may demonstrate. Clearly, if females had a lower commitment to teaching as a long-term career than their male counterparts, then a lower rate of promotion must be expected. The second variable relates to differential motivations and attitudes that might cause female teachers to be less anxious to seek or accept administrative positions.

With respect to the commitment issue, it has long been accepted on the basis of historic evidence that many women enter teaching as a stopgap between the completion of their own education and anticipated nuptials. While some failed to marry and a few returned after child-rearing (though at one time there were strictures against married women continuing to teach), the majority were assumed to be temporary practitioners and hence not likely to gain the experience necessary for promotion to administrative levels. However, with the escalation of educational requirements for licensing and the current prevalence of dual-income marriages such assumptions need to be seriously examined.

In this regard it is noteworthy that as early as 1955 female teachers had, on average, nearly half a year more teaching experience than did their male counterparts. While this may have been a lingering consequence of the wartime distortions, the experience norms of male teachers did not catch up until 1970 when both males and females averaged just over seven years of experience. Male teachers gained a small advantage by 1980 when their eleven-year career average exceeded the female average by one year (SC 81-568, 81-569). However, as discussed elsewhere, these more recent career-attachment data suggest that any tendency for women teachers to leave teaching early is better understood as a reaction to, rather than a cause of, their blocked mobility. In any event, it should be clear that the evidence over the last quarter-century has not supported the assumption that the low proportion of women teachers in positions of added responsibility is explainable in terms of their lower career commitment.

While there is little in the way of relevant data that pre-dates the recent rise in social concern over gender inequity, Eichler's (1979–80) survey of Toronto teachers regarding their 'sex-role attitudes' is revealing of the current attitudinal differences between male and female teachers regarding promotion to administrative roles. In this study, a set of 'is' versus 'ought' questions was specifically developed to test teachers' 'attitudes towards women and men in authority positions.' The results clearly demonstrate that women teachers not only recognize the magnitude of the current gender inequality in educational administration (95 per cent), but they even more strongly believe (97.9 per cent) that women should be given greater opportunities to take on leadership roles. Male teachers, while recognizing the existence of the inequalities (83 per cent), were significantly less willing to concede the need for reform (73.1 per cent). When asked whether it made a difference to them whether they had a male or female supervisor, only 15 per cent of the women but 30 per cent of the men indicated that they preferred a male. Interestingly, there was very little difference between males (68.7 per cent) and females (69.7 per cent) in their judgment of whether women were as achievement-oriented in their teaching careers as men.

On the basis of these data it would appear that deeply entrenched institutional norms and practices, not self-deprecating attitudes on the part of female teachers, are responsible for the extraordinarily low proportion of women teachers who occupied administrative positions through to at least the mid-1980s.

ETHNICITY

That Canada is a pluralistic society willing, like its southern neighbour, to absorb an ethnically diverse population has been an article of national faith. But unlike America's image of itself as a 'melting-pot' out of which uniform national character traits are to be cast,

Canadians are widely believed to value a multicultural 'mosaic' within which ethnic differences are celebrated. Whatever the reality of the American melting-pot versus the Canadian mosaic, John Porter's (1965) seminal study of Canada's social, economic, and political structure suggests that the nation's ethnic pluralism is primarily oriented to the British and French 'charter groups.' Given this, the question of ethnic over- or under-representation among teachers relative to the population as a whole needs to be considered in relation to the French/Anglo 'Charter Groups' and with respect to all other ethnic minorities.

With regard to the bicultural dimension, the dominant cultural socialization role which the schools have been assigned (Dreeban 1977) would imply not only proportional French/Anglo representation in the Canadian teacher labour-force, but a strong commitment to ethnic dualism within the whole structure of Canadian public education. There is indeed much evidence to support the view that historically Canada's 'two solitudes' maintained highly distinctive educational systems in which cultural factors clearly dominated. For example, Lamontagne (1977) has argued that traditionally in Quebec the control of French language education by the Roman Catholic church, along with the 'classical' character of the elite schools, undoubtedly served to ensure cultural 'valorization.' However, after the rapid secularization of education that accompanied the 'quiet revolution,' the Quebec public school system, except in its approach to language issues, came into close conformity with the North American norm.

At the other extreme, the Anglo cultural character of public education in English-speaking Canada was until relatively recently perhaps most strongly pursued in Ontario. Indeed, as Fleming (1971) has noted, as recently as the 1970 School Administration Act there existed a specific legal restriction on the granting of permanent Ontario teaching certificates only to 'British subjects of good moral character' (Section 19). While this restriction was not so binding as to preclude the temporary licensing of those who had already applied to become 'British subjects,' or who declared their intention of becoming a Canadian citizen when eligible, the ethnic bias was nevertheless obvious.

If the 1960s produced the 'quiet revolution' of secular modernization in Quebec, the 1970s and 1980s saw a no less profound reassessment of cultural pluralism in English-speaking Canada. As a consequence, not only have the public education policies in the English-speaking provinces recognized their obligations with respect to promoting a bilingual society, major efforts have been made to reverse the cultural genocide policies which Brant (1977) has so cogently documented with respect to Canada's native people.

Public education in Canada would appear to have become simultaneously more convergent in its approaches to core structures and curricula and more accepting of divergence in culturally relevant electives, especially language options. The net effect of this trend upon the teacher work-force will almost inevitably see increasing emphasis on ethnically proportional recruitment. Greater effort to extend such recruitment into rural ethnic communities may also be anticipated so as to remedy the heretofore abysmal shortage of school personnel in remote areas.

However, as things currently stand, ethnic proportionality has yet to be achieved within the established teaching-force. While there is no reliable official source of data on teacher ethnicity, a national survey of all employed Canadians conducted by members of the Department of Sociology at Carleton University (1983) included a specific ethnicity identification item. The wording of the interview question was: 'To what ethnic or cultural group did you or your ancestors (on the male side) belong on coming to this continent?' (Q. 169). A special run on this data base was undertaken in order to create a sub-sample file of public school teachers. Table 3.3 compares the proportion of Canadian teachers who identified themselves as members of either of the two charter groups with their overall societal proportions (1971 census data).

As is readily apparent, teachers originating from the United Kingdom are approximately ten percentage points over-represented relative to their overall population proportion, while teachers with French origins are under-represented in the same amount. It is impossible to determine on the basis of available data the extent to which this disproportionality reflects differing participation rates and student-teacher ratios associated with each of the two language groups, or the extent to which French students outside of Quebec receive instruction predominantly from Anglo teachers.

So far as the non-charter ethnic groups are concerned, the available data are inconclusive except in the case of native Canadians, who remain the most educationally deprived ethnic group in the nation (Hull 1987). While major efforts are now under way to rectify this situation, including compensatory recruitment and preparation of native teachers, it will no doubt take some time before past neglect is overcome.

SOCIO-ECONOMIC ORIGINS

Although the legitimacy of all so-called open liberal-democratic societies is predicated to a significant degree upon the presumption of no structural barriers to social mobility, sociological analysis invariably reveals that the socio-economic status (SES) of the family strongly influences an individual's choice of occupation. But having noted this propensity to inherit one's 'life chances,' it is also important to recognize that intergenerational mobility, both up and down the occupational hierarchy, regularly occurs and that certain occupations have proved to be better avenues of social mobility than others.

In this regard, schoolteaching is unique among the knowledge-based occupations in that all those who could possibly qualify are, by virtue of their prior exposure as students, well aware of both the essential character of the work and the qualification criteria. This visibility stands in sharp contrast to that of more elite professions that have such narrow exposure that the majority of those coming from less-than-privileged backgrounds are likely to be substantially ignorant of what the job entails and how entry may be gained. It has been widely assumed therefore that teaching has been and remains an attractive avenue of upward mobility for those from lower SES origins. These generalizations need to be examined carefully in light of historic and contemporary evidence.

In the United States, where mobility studies have been better developed for a longer period than in Canada, the conventional presumption that teaching is an avenue of upward mobility is verified only with regard to males. In reporting the extensive data on teacher backgrounds accumulated by the National Education Association, Lortie (1975:34) notes that at least 30 per cent of the U.S. teachers came from blue-collar families. Given this, Lortie concludes that 'teaching appears to be one of the more important routes into the middle class' (35). But, as he also notes, 'Men and women do not benefit equally from these mobility gains' (35). For whatever reason, female teachers have come, on average, from significantly higher social origins than their male counterparts.

British social mobility studies reveal a similar pattern of below-mean SES recruitment for males and above-mean SES recruitment for females. But as Floud and Scott (1961) warned, the traditional over-representation of working-class origin males within the teacher labour-force showed evidence of diminishing by the end of the 1950s.

In Canada, Jones (1963) was among the first to test the upward mobility potential of the teaching profession. Using a sample of Hamilton teachers, Jones reached similar conclusions: i.e., when controlled for age, there was 'a steady increase [to 1960] in the accessibility of teaching to persons of lower social origin' (237); but when controlled for gender, 'the greater proportion of men is found among teachers of lowest social origin, while the greater proportion of women is found among teachers of higher social origin' (240).

More recent studies conducted by the Department of Educational Research at the University of Toronto (reported by Watson, Quazi & Poyntz 1972) on the social origins of Ontario secondary school teacher-trainees verify in the Canadian context, the results of a study of teacher recruitment trends in Britain by Floud and Scott (1961). The first of these Ontario studies was conducted in 1959, with a replication in 1964. Both surveys classified the parental origins of the teacher-trainees in terms of the father's basic occupational category. The results, which are depicted graphically in Figures 3.2 and 3.3, show that by 1964 there was a clear departure from the historic social-origin pattern. In the 1959 survey the male distribution within the overall bimodal pattern is symmetrical around the blue-collar parental occupational category. By 1964, however, it had become symmetrical around the semi-professional category. Again, by 1964, the bimodal pattern of females, which in 1959 still had the largest segment coming from upper middle-class professional and executive families, had moved downward to meet the upwardly shifting male pattern. These studies reveal that teaching, at least at the secondary level in Ontario, was moving away from its historic intergenerational mobility pattern to one which conformed much more closely to the normal intergenerational social-inheritance pattern.

In order to obtain an even more up-to-date national verification of this Ontario trend, a special run was made of three successive national post-secondary student-population surveys conducted during the 1968/9, 1974/5, and 1982/3 academic years. Table 3.4 summarizes the results. The traditional teacher-mobility pattern is apparent in the 1969 data. Male teacher-education students in that year were three times under-represented at the highest parent-occupation category level and one-and-one-half times over-represented at the lowest level when compared to all other university students. However, female teacher-education students in the same 1969 group were proportionally twice as numerous as their male counterparts in the higher SES origin category, while being notably less associated with the lowest social-origin group.

By 1975, however, the numbers of male and female teacher-education students were equivalent, and by 1983 the social-origin distribution of teacher-education students was in almost perfect conformity with the 'all other' student social-origin profile. Since this 'all other' university student profile is strongly skewed toward the middle- and upper-middle-class end of the SES spectrum, the more recent data leave no doubt that schoolteaching in Canada is not the avenue of social mobility that it once was and is still assumed to be.

Various reasons for this 'regression toward the mean' may be posed. For example, Floud and Scott's (1961) British study, which applied to teachers at all levels, noted that the critical change occurred during a period of escalating educational requirements for teacher certification. They speculated that this fact alone could explain the reduction in working-class recruitment. Since numerous studies have documented the extent to which those from working-class origins tend to be significantly under-represented among the college-going population, such a conjecture seems reasonable. However, this was also a period in which Canadian teacher salaries, presumably influenced by both the teacher shortage and the rising social value assigned to education, significantly increased. It was also a period when other employment markets for university graduates began to decline (Harvey 1974). It is reasonable therefore to suspect that during the 1970s secondary-level teaching crossed the established middle-class acceptability threshold as a legitimate occupational aspiration for males.

As for the decline in the traditional over-representation of women from higher-status family backgrounds, the previous discussion of what certainly appears to be retarded gender-equity promotion practices within the teaching career system offers some obvious explanation. Clearly, women who come from families in an advantageous position to facilitate their pursuing of better opportunities that lie elsewhere are likely to do just that.

AGE STRUCTURE

A number of factors influence the age profile of any occupation's incumbent work-force. These include:

1 The effects of expansion or contraction upon the ratio of new-entrant inflow to retirement outflow.
2 The comparative state of relative advantage between competing occupational markets that may recruit from each other.
3 The age specificity of the work itself.
4 The existence of recruitment norms that may discriminate against early, middle, or late working-life entry.
5 The extent to which retirement regulations or pension arrangements encourage or discourage early, normal, or late retirement.
6 The degree to which the occupation is attractive as a lifelong career or perceived as a stepping-stone to some other occupational destination.
7 Whether the promotion and/or job enlargement opportunities are sufficient to maintain the interest of the more capable incumbents.
8 The incentive characteristics of the remuneration formula, e.g., whether incremental by seniority or performance and/or whether the overall career earnings are front- or end-loaded.

Recalling the earlier discussion of market-versus-institutional career factors, items 1 and 2 may be seen as primarily market-driven, whereas items 3 through 8 are primarily determined by institutional factors, such as policy directives and career norms.

With respect to the market variables, teaching shares a common age-compositional dynamic with most other occupational sectors. Specifically, under long-term steady-state conditions where the new-entrant cohort exactly balances the retirement cohort, the age composition within the occupation should be 'normal,' that is to say, evenly distributed across the full working-age spectrum. However, under conditions of expansion where new-entrant intake exceeds retirement outflow, the overall work-force will inevitably become youth-skewed, that is to say, the age of the average worker will fall. By the same token, should the demand-factor decline after a period of rapid expansion, the work-force will age until the initial youth bulge is transformed into a pre-retirement bulge.

Because of the rapid cycling in teacher demand that occurred with the shift in fertility rates over the past few decades, on the basis of demand factors alone the teacher work-force was bound to experience a progressive shift from a younger to an older age profile. This age distortion was then exacerbated by the second market factor, i.e., the teaching profession's competitive position relative to other careers. In essence, at the time when teacher demand was expanding most rapidly there was a general increase in demand for workers with similar educational backgrounds. As a consequence, a relatively high rate of early- to mid-career mobility out of teaching into other occupations occurred. This could only increase the youth-distortion effect as even younger replacements were hired. However, by the time the demographic factors were working in the opposite direction and all but eliminating the hiring of youthful new-entrants, the opportunities to make a mid-career shift out of teaching had also been severely curtailed. This, in turn, served to reinforce the collective aging effect by further limiting the need to hire young replacements.

Given that these market factors were essentially non-controllable, we need to examine whether the more controllable institutional factors were brought into play through such offsetting policy interventions as age-target recruitment, altered incentive packages, and early-retirement arrangements.

One such institutionally controllable factor already referred to is the flexibility in education standards for entry into the teacher-training institutions. Clearly, the relatively low entry standards of the past reflected the desperate need to recruit new teachers. By the same token the abrupt introduction of dramatically higher teacher-training entry standards appears as a relatively crude 'gatekeeping' response to earlier planning failures. This is not, of course, to argue that such high standards are not beneficial in the long term. However, their very abrupt invocation at the point where new-entrant teacher surpluses were becoming an embarrassment strongly suggests a somewhat more cynical motivation. But such a reactive labour-adjustment instrument only promises to reproduce the boom/bust market cycling of the past. What seems not to have been much considered are more 'elastic' career adjustments aimed at offsetting the age distortion effect that alternating open and closed recruitment policies inevitably produces. For example, during the rapid expansion period, virtually all the effort to recruit staff for the expanding classrooms was focused on youthful new-entrants. This policy not only failed to recognize the 'time bomb' implications of such a massive age-compositional distortion but also the institutional-stability values that would have accrued if personnel policies had focused more upon mid-career retention and recruitment. Nor was there any real justification offered as to why there were so many financial and institutional disincentives imposed upon those relatively few older, and in many cases, highly subject-qualified individuals who did enter teaching without teacher-training qualifications via the teacher-shortage-engendered 'letter of permission' route. Unless such individuals were prepared to go through the pro forma teacher-training ritual, they were given their walking papers just as soon as younger 'qualified' recruits became available. But there is little in the considerable research literature on the value of teacher-training that would support the conclusion that such formal preparation is any more predictive of teaching success (or failure) than on-the-job experience. The question must therefore be asked in retrospect, why couldn't those more mature individuals who arrived in the classroom by unconventional paths and who demonstrated high aptitude and commitment not have been encouraged to stay on, and in so doing provide more age balance? After all, the engineering societies make provision for the bestowing of professional status upon those who demonstrate their competence through on-the-job experience rather than university graduation.

Other more subtle institutional disincentives to age-balancing were and are operant. For example, the limitation on job-enlargement at the classroom level and the absence of performance-related incentives and recognition in combination with an early maximized pay-scale serve to discourage mid-career retention and recruitment. Had there been more incentives aimed at maximizing rather than minimizing mid-career satisfactions invoked during the expansionary period, there would undoubtedly have been a much higher proportion of retirement-age teachers leaving the system precisely at the time when enrolment declines would have made such 'natural attrition' most desirable.

However, since this kind of fine-tuned approach to labour-force planning has not occurred, we may anticipate recurrences of the teacher supply/demand problem. As indicated in the review of population forecasts, there will continue to be some short-cycle instability in the school population resulting from both the more predictable demographic and the less predictable economic and social variables. The first of these 'blips' is already heralding an immanent, if brief, period of teacher shortage. But having all but closed the entry gate, it will be difficult to justify flinging it open again, especially if in so doing the age-distortion cycle is only reproduced.

Support for this analysis of the age-distortion dilemma facing the teaching profession is clearly manifest in the statistical evidence. Table 3.5 provides the essential mean-age and median-experience data, as available, for the period between 1955 and 1983.[1] By comparing the change in mean-age and median experience with the change in demand, it is apparent that the demographically driven demand factor is strongly related to the teacher age/experience compositional profile.

However, these central tendency comparisons do not reveal the full extent to which the long period of expansion, in combination with a high level of mid-career attrition, has created an age-composition inertia that, for some time to come, will place the majority of teachers in the lower age cohorts. Figure 3.4 provides a graphic comparison of the cohort age-distribution of the 1972/3, 1977/8, and 1983/4 teacher labour-forces. As is readily apparent, though the mean age peak has moved toward the mid-career age-level, the proportion of teachers approaching normal retirement age remains disproportionately small. Indeed, if we divide a career-span of approximately 45 years into three divisions – those under 34 years old, those between 35 and 49, and those over 50 – and then compare the change in proportion of the teacher labour-force which occupies each division over the decade after the enrolments began to decline (Table 3.6), three features become immediately apparent. First, the proportion of the total teacher labour-force within the

1 Unfortunately, Statistics Canada's annual education survey underwent a methodological change in 1972 which precludes age comparisons prior to that date. However, there is full historical data on median years of teaching experience, from which age patterns may be inferred.

under-34 'new-entrant' division was cut nearly in half. Second, the proportion of teachers in the 'pre-retirement,' over-50 division remained constant at 12 per cent (±1%) through the decade and will not reach a normal proportionality until the mid-1990s. Third, most teachers had arrived at, or were close to, the top of the front-loaded salary scale, so that further aging would not significantly alter the total teacher-salary bill.

Thus, unless there are some radical changes in the institutional factors which encourage a more normally distributed age profile, the teacher labour-force will collectively age at close to one year annually until the current median-age peak reaches retirement age toward the first decade of the next century. At this point the teacher labour-force may be expected to rejuvenate itself rapidly and, as noted above, reproduce the age-composition distortion once again, unless there is some serious rethinking of the policies and practices that affect the teaching career structure.

EDUCATIONAL ATTAINMENTS

Although teachers are the most visible ambassadors of the public education establishment, they have not always exemplified the system's highest level of scholarly attainment. A university degree has always been considered desirable for secondary-level teaching, but it has not been a requirement for elementary teachers until quite recently. Indeed, for elementary teachers, high-school graduation was not even a requirement in many jurisdictions until after the Second World War, and through the 1950s fully one-third of the nation's secondary teachers functioned without bachelor's level certification.

However, as Table 3.7 shows, recruitment and in-service upgrading practices that emphasized higher educational attainments resulted in a rapid increase in the proportion of teachers with university degrees at all levels after 1960. The proportion of all teachers who earned master's or higher degrees, while remaining relatively small, also increased significantly from 2.3 per cent in 1960 to 10 per cent by 1983 (SC 81-202, 81-568).

Although the upgrading of the educational requirements of teachers has often been linked with the post-war 'knowledge explosion,' the fact that many teachers, even at the secondary level, often teach subjects well-removed from their own educational specialties suggests that other factors may also be involved. For example, the availability of university graduates grew very rapidly after 1960. Although part of this growth was demographically determined, a major component was the exponential increase in the university participation rates. In response to this increase in the supply of graduates, Berg (1970), Folger and Nam (1964), and Harvey (1974) documented how 'credential inflation' – a term applied to the escalation of educational requirements beyond the actual job requisites – became a common feature of the overall labour-market. This over-supply resulted in a situation which degraded the ordinary bachelor's degree to much the same occupational pre-requisite category formerly occupied by the high-school diploma.

But if the ordinary first degree was becoming what Marien (1971:16) unflatteringly termed 'a postindustrial puberty rite,' those who earned it, at least initially, failed to lower their occupational expectations accordingly. As a result, the supply of those with general degrees outstripped the demand in most of the managerial or semi-professional categories. The exception was teaching which, during the baby-boom period, was not only expanding at unprecedented rates but, unlike most other formally licensed occupations, did not then require either high levels of academic achievement or carefully pre-planned undergraduate programs.

As a consequence, Lortie's (1975) comprehensive survey of U.S. schoolteachers identified those who entered teaching as being predominantly attracted on the basis of some combination of 'blocked aspirations' and easy 'convertibility' (49). That some individuals cannot attain their first-choice occupational aspirations is, of course, not unusual. However, this 'easy convertibility' characteristic of teaching is most certainly unique within the formally licensed professional occupations. While most North American teacher-training faculties provide a more complete professional-development option in the form of a full undergraduate pedagogy degree, they also offer a one-year BEd conversion that can be added on to virtually any other degree (Koerner 1963; Roth 1983).

By comparing the proportion of university students who declared an education major from the outset of their undergraduate careers to those who took the one-year add-on program after graduating in another field, it is possible to infer the extent to which teaching became a fall-back option. Data from the 1969 and 1976

Post-secondary Graduate Survey (Picot 1983) show that although 50.4 per cent of all the employed 1969 graduates of Canadian universities had become teachers by 1971, only 20.8 per cent had declared early majors in pedagogy. A similar survey conducted in 1978 with respect to 1976 graduates reveals virtually the same proportion of early-committed students (20.7 per cent) but a decline to 41.2 per cent of the total university-graduating cohort who were teaching by 1978. The 10 per cent reduction no doubt reflects the change in the teacher-demand that occurred between the two survey dates.

The same data base provides insights into the fields of study from which these education 'converts' come. Table 3.8 summarizes the findings. As might be expected, those who pursued undergraduate programs in fine arts or humanities, or who were general degree majors, became easy converts to teaching after graduating into a labour-market that had become increasingly resistant and that was undoubtedly using educational specialization criteria as an initial screening device. However, the notably high rates of entry from social sciences, biological sciences, agriculture, mathematics, and physical sciences also suggest that teaching became the fall-back career option among the more instrumentally trained who were not able or willing to pursue their specialty to a postgraduate degree or more demanding professional level.

These university graduate surveys, bracketing as they do the peak of the school-expansion period, demonstrate the truly exceptional degree to which teaching was able to absorb the exponentially expanding university-graduate population. However, they do not provide a longer-term view of the shift in occupational destination for graduates or indicate how other occupational fields were responding to the increase in highly qualified manpower.

A special run of the Highly Qualified Manpower (1973) survey of a sample of all university graduates to 1973 provides some of these insights. Table 3.9 shows the proportion of all university graduates who entered teaching as their first full-time job, as well as other occupational fields that traditionally employ graduates. The distributions are broken down by graduating cohorts (5-year intervals) from the 1950s on, and are controlled for the highest degree level obtained. The comparison reveals that between 1950 and 1970 all employment sectors except schoolteaching and university and college employment (teaching at another level) showed a decline in the proportion of newly available graduates hired. School-teaching, however, *doubled its proportional recruitment of new graduates*, and the universities and colleges nearly doubled their proportional employment of master's-level graduates and continued to monopolize doctoral-level graduates.

These data clearly show the extent to which the public education system absorbed almost all the rapid increase in the post-secondary output. There is an element of self-fulfilling prophecy in this, given the frequency with which the 'demand' for graduates was cited by educationalists and others as cause for further expansion of the education system! Had the baby-boom aberration not presented itself in such a way as to provide convenient fall-back employment opportunities for the burgeoning supply of university graduates, the recognition of the limits on demand for highly qualified manpower probably would have come much sooner than it did.

This absorption of occupationally displaced graduates into the teaching-ranks was facilitated not only by the easy convertibility arrangements of teacher-training institutions, but also by the teacher-training philosophy which elevated pedagogic 'methodology' above substantive subject knowledge as the principal ingredient in the professional preparation of teachers. Given this philosophy, it didn't much matter what the academic background of those who came to the teacher-training faculties might be. Since it is the professional-training element which represents the common core which all properly licensed teachers share, this component of their education obviously deserves some special consideration.

TEACHER-TRAINING INSTITUTIONS

The 1960s saw a major transformation in the locus of teacher-training in Canada. Until then, provincial ministries of education operated 'normal schools' for the sole purpose of preparing teachers for classroom duty. The shift from these in-house operations to education faculties within universities, where education degrees are granted at bachelor's, master's, and doctoral levels, followed a wider trend toward the integration of all professional training within the broader mandate of the university. This removal of teacher-training (but not licensing authority) from the direct control of the public education bureaucracy was heralded at the time as a major triumph in the struggle for full professional status, but the victory has so far remained only partial. The frustrating limitation that remains lies in the persisting problem that education faculties have had convincing other disciplines within the hallowed halls that they are capable of meeting the academic standards of the more established members of the university federation.

In part, these academic legitimacy difficulties are characteristic of all professional-training faculties which must try to rationalize their more self-serving and externally defined knowledge criteria with the university's long-established commitment to institutional autonomy and the 'disinterested pursuit of knowledge.' As Calam (1977) has argued, to the extent that education faculties serve the 'instrumental skill development' and 'indoctrination' requisites of government-controlled licensing bodies, they confound the most hallowed norms of academic purity as well as risk the charge of triviality. But to the extent that they adopt the academic 'knowledge for its own sake' norms and meet the publishing expectations of the more autonomous faculties, they must confront their own constituencies' charge of 'irrelevance.'

Even if some irreconcilable tension between applied and basic scholarship is inevitable, the evidence to date strongly suggests that the professional training of teachers has not been particularly effective – even when measured against the more narrowly defined professional-training criteria. For example, Koerner (1963) offers but faint praise of American faculties of education when he describes them as a 'sincere, humanitarian, well-intentioned, hard-working, poorly informed, badly educated and ineffectual group of men and women' (37). Similarly, Wolf (1984) talks of excessive instrumentalism and Marien (1971) of dysfunctional credentialism. In Britain, Taylor (1965) assessed education faculties as 'small, inadequately staffed, badly housed and held in poor regard within the university ... [and by] student opinion' (193). In Canada, Nash (1962) complains of the 'monumental triviality' of the main body of education-faculty research that, despite the improvements noted by the Canadian Education Association, had still to satisfy a Queen's University report which warned of 'overworked faculty, swindled graduate students, social pressures and academic prostitution' (Calam 1977:142–3).

As with all such blanket evaluations, there are many notable exceptions, as evidenced by some of the truly innovative research produced by education faculty and their graduate students. Nevertheless, so much consistent criticism from so many quarters cannot go unexamined.

The most obvious source of the academic quality problem lies in the timing of the transfer of teacher-training into the university. This move coincided with the period of rapid school-system expansion. With the demand for teachers far outstripping the available supply, the pressure to keep teacher-training entry and exit standards relatively low – in most instances, a minimal pass grade in virtually any major subject area – was irresistible. While many of those who opted to become teachers were high achievers, many more were not. No doubt such minimal selection criteria contributed to the problems teachers experienced in achieving greater professional recognition.

However, the rapid shift in the teacher supply-demand ratio from deficit to surplus has had a profound effect on teacher-training admission standards. By the mid-1980s, virtually all of Canada's education faculties brought their standards into line with the other professional faculties by requiring honours-level grades for program admission. It will be some time yet before an assessment can be made of what effect these more select recruits will have on an occupation that for some years to come will remain dominated by those who have been less rigorously recruited. Nor is it yet possible to predict in what way, if at all, these new admission standards will affect the academic standards and attitudes of teacher-training faculty themselves. Certainly, the recent shift from quantity to quality in selection of students would encourage members of education faculties to shift their own performance norms away from the imperatives of mass training toward greater emphasis on quality research. Should this occur, education faculties may yet provide the distinctive combination of practical knowledge and humanistic values upon which the professional claims and aspirations of their students ultimately depend.[2]

But given the earlier discussion of the relatively weak professional context within which teachers currently pursue their careers, it is by no means clear that education faculties will succeed in becoming effective agents of professional training and socializa-

---

2 In this respect, it is interesting to reflect on the positive effect upon the professional status of medical practitioners resulting from the reforms in medical education and research that occurred earlier this century.

tion, even if they do manage to become recognized as centres of academic excellence. There is overwhelming evidence (e.g., Battersby 1983; Gregory 1976, 1978; Newberry 1979; Page 1983; Pierce 1974; Ratsoy 1966) that it is perceptions of their own past student experiences in combination with the 'practicum' internship phase of their training that is the strongest source of occupational socialization among teacher trainees. If this is true, then the often-expressed concern that teachers lack appropriate professional value references needs to be examined.

VALUE ORIENTATIONS AND PRAGMATIC PRACTICES

As noted in Chapter One, researchers have identified a contradiction common to most of the human-service professions, i.e., the dichotomy between the ideology of altruistic humanism, which typically motivates those seeking entry to a profession, and the instrumental authoritarianism that tends to dominate the professional-practice environment (e.g., Ference et al 1973; Hall 1948; Lortie 1959; Montagna 1973). Studies reveal that this dichotomy is usually resolved in favour of the authoritarian operational practice norms which focus almost exclusively upon the instrumentalities of intentionally, and often excessively, closed systems of knowledge during the professional-training experience (Becker & Geer 1958; Hall 1948).

While medical schools have been identified as the ultimate example of this triumph of the instrumental over the humanistic orientation in their establishment of the practitioner's unassailable authority, all professions seek some similar field of technical knowledge as the basis of their claim to professional status. But, as suggested earlier, the only unique form of instrumental knowledge upon which teachers can lay an equivalent claim to professional authority is that of 'teaching methodology.' Given this, it is not surprising that education faculties tend to emphasize this aspect of teacher-training. Whatever the real value of this instrumentalism may be, the credibility of claims that such formally acquired training in pedagogic technique is the absolute criterion for successful professional practice is seriously undercut by two factors. First, there is the widely observed fact that virtually all those engaged in post-secondary teaching (ironically, including many of those who teach teachers) do not have such formal pedagogic training.

Second, while it may be argued that children represent a clientele sufficiently unique as to warrant professionals who have been specially trained, those who have had such training have not been overly generous in crediting it as an important factor in preparing them for their subsequent teaching roles. Indeed, when surveyed on the subject, teachers tend to identify subject knowledge and personality factors, such as their attitudes toward students, as the most critical factors in classroom performance.

Perhaps because formal pedagogic training has not been clearly established as the prime element through which successful practice is achieved, education faculties typically include a significant number of 'student-centred' humanists who encourage the opposite of instrumentalism, that is, a student-centred approach to intellectual development. Presumably, this attempt to achieve some balance between the authoritarian logic of instrumentalism and the empathic logic of a liberal-humanistic pedagogic philosophy offers teacher-trainees a real choice of approaches which should find subsequent expression in their classrooms (Calam 1977; Macdonald 1970).

But even if teacher-trainees do perceive such a choice, there is strong evidence that what is learned in the formal instructional component of the professional training experience has not contributed significantly to professional socialization. Given this evidence, the questions that need to be asked with respect to the relationship between teacher-training and professional socialization are of two kinds. First, what are the relative strengths of the preparatory socialization undertaken by faculties of education and what Turner (1964) has identified as the hidden persuaders of 'anticipatory socialization'? Second, how is the actual practice of teaching, as opposed to its idealized theory, determined? Stated in terms of our concern for the professional status of teachers, these questions translate into whether teachers, in general, come to perceive the basis of their professional authority and institutional support as being more securely rooted in acting as agents in the transmission of highly structured and externally sanctioned knowledge or in acting as facilitators of a more client-centred pursuit of critical awareness and judgments.

Whatever the intellectual interest pedagogic theories may have for teacher-trainees, it is how one performs during the short, but intensive, practice-teaching period that is correctly understood by most candidates as the critical test upon which licensing and employment opportunities depend (Gregory & Allen 1978; Nutter 1983; Page 1983). Not surprisingly, for student teachers, who are under the duress of having to demonstrate short-term performance capabilities that are evaluated by an in-service teacher and in front of an already organizationally conditioned student clientele, it is existing practices rather than idealistic alternatives that must carry the day.

Yet, as Loosemore and Carlton's (1977) study warns, not only is the practicum experience intrinsically unrepresentative of the normal classroom situation, it may also engender some very real inhibitions to full professional development. This is so precisely because the student-teacher may fixate on the 'dramaturgical' role sets that the contrived situation produces. Since the 'drama' is largely played out in accordance with the mutually perceived necessity for maintaining behavioural control (even a momentary loss of which represents the greatest fear of both the student and host teacher), it is not surprising that the manifest instrumentality of the formal lesson-plan and the latent authoritarianism of a didactic teaching style tend to be powerfully reinforced at the expense of even the most strongly held student-centred personal values.

All this suggests that despite any commitment to liberal humanistic values manifested during the teacher-training experience, and notwithstanding the large body of evidence identifying the most successful teachers as having non-threatening, empathic pedagogic styles and an open-ended, inquiring approach to their subject-matter (e.g., Hamachek 1969; Spady 1977), the dominant professional practice norms under which schoolteaching functions, especially within the secondary division, will continue to reflect, though likely with increasing cynicism, instrumental, authoritarian values.

Hodgett's (1968) study of how Canadian teachers approach the issue of 'civic' understanding is a salient example of this kind of cynical acceptance of instrumental pedagogy. After surveying a national sample of high-school teachers and witnessing a number of classroom situations, Hodgett concluded:

The evidence suggests that, as teachers of difficult subjects in a complex society, their thinking will be fuzzy and superficial. They will follow the rules and regulations so rigidly that, in actual fact, they will be misinter-preting and abusing some of the good advice they have received in teacher-training institutions ... The textbook is a convenient crutch; the doctrine that it does not matter what we teach provides a golden excuse to play around with teaching tactics divorced from content; or conversely, the simple, unimaginative question-answer technique of the assignment method is an easy escape from quality work in the classroom. (107)

King and Ripton (1970) provide further evidence of the deeply rooted instrumental practices that motivate teachers prior to taking up their careers. Utilizing a stratified sample of in-service high-school teachers, pre-service teacher-trainees, and high-school students in southern Ontario, the study found that '78 per cent of the [in-service] teachers from the interview sample responded with statements couched in the ideological idiom of creativity, freedom, responsibility and student-centredness' (42). However, when asked to identify what comprises effective teaching, 'less than five per cent of the teachers employed similar terms to those they employed in describing the purpose of education' (43). As a consequence, the authors concluded that 'teachers do in fact maintain an ideological conception of the purpose of education that is far removed from their operational definition of the act of teaching. Curricula derived from their ideological statements would be substantially different from those assumed in their descriptions of the good teacher' (43).

In search of an explanation of this contradiction, King and Ripton found that anticipatory socialization among both the student-teacher and in-service teacher samples reinforced the instru-mental-authoritarian practice over the liberal-humanistic ideology. When asked what they expected to be doing fifteen years from now, over 80 per cent of both the student teachers and in-service teach-ers expected to be either in a higher-status occupation or promoted to administration. When asked to define the personal characteris-tics required to be a good teacher and then a good administrator, the liberal-humanistic responses were strongly associated with the teaching role, whereas the instrumental-authoritarian responses were strongly associated with the administrative role.

This instrumental orientation of teachers also found expression in the responses of a sample of their high-school students, over 90 per cent of whom gave instrumental responses to the question seeking their perceptions of what was most valuable in getting an education. These same students also seemed to have accepted their teachers' definition of their institutionally defined learning and behaviour predispositions, i.e., that they were 'collectively irresponsible,' 'asocial,' and requiring 'control' – all of which, if true, would certainly provide justification for instrumental and authoritarian approaches to teaching.

But if 'teacher expectations' are as powerful a source of student achievement and behaviour motivation as Rosenthal and Jacobson (1966, 1968) have demonstrated, and if the effects of a school's administrative philosophy are as deterministic of the attitudes of students toward their education as Nordstrom, Friedenberg, and Gold's (1967) study suggests, then clearly it cannot be assumed that the students' own school-related self-perceptions and behaviour are separable from those of their teachers and administrative staff.

However, in comparing Hodgetts's (1968) with King and Ripton's (1970) interpretation of the dominant mode of classroom instructional practice, it is apparent that while there is significant agreement as to what actually takes place, Hodgetts imputes a personal-value explanation, whereas King and Ripton identify institutional factors as the primary source of the predominant instrumental-authoritarian orientation. In order to test these explanations further, a special run was made on the Carleton University (1983) Canadian Class Structure Project data base. This representative national survey of employed Canadians, which was conducted in the winter of 1982–3, presents nineteen items through which a comparison of value orientation between practising teachers and other occupational groups can be factored out. For our purposes, the respondents were partitioned into three occupational groupings: all currently employed school 'Teachers,' all others in the 'Managerial and Professional' category, and a residual of predominantly 'Hourly Paid Employees.'

The results are presented in Table 3.10. A comparison of the column means reveals that the proportion of teachers with strong authoritarian orientations is significantly smaller than for either the 'Hourly' or the 'Managerial and Professional' groups. Such a finding hardly supports the assumption that an exceptionally large number of Canadian teachers come to their work with authoritarian personal values. What this comparison does reveal, however, is that while having no higher proportion of strong liberals than the working population as a whole, teachers do have a much higher proportion of 'middle-of-the-roaders' (nearly 62 per cent compared with 58 per cent for Managerial and Professional, and 55 per cent for Hourly employees). What this in turn implies is that, other factors being equal, teachers would in practice favour the values of the strong liberals, who outnumber strong authoritarians by nearly two to one. However, the institutional factors are apparently effective in orienting the large 'no strong opinion' majority toward the bureaucratically favoured instrumental-authoritarian pattern that so many have found characteristic of the pedagogical practices of Canadian teachers.

Having noted this general situation, it is nevertheless interesting to observe some of the contradictions within the predominant value orientations of teachers. An item-by-item comparison shows teachers, in comparison with the other groups, to be less conservative in their views on the sources of poverty and more liberal in their support for welfare-transfer payments and in questioning the universal value of profit motivation. These characteristics may be attributed to the fact that almost all teachers work within the public sector, whereas a good proportion of the workers in the other two categories are employed in the private sector, where institutional ideology tends to be more conservative on these issues. However, with the notable exception of one item, teachers differ very little from the other occupational categories in their views on crime and punishment. But the one anomalous item in this area is revealing. Teachers are considerably more conservative in their belief that crime would be reduced if children were in general subjected to greater discipline. This suggests that teachers either feel they do not have the proper resources to pursue the 'social control' role they are expected to play, or that the standards of discipline expected in the school are not reflected in the wider society. Although beyond the scope of this inquiry, there is ample prima facie evidence to suggest that both possibilities obtain. If so, this may leave teachers feeling insecure, or vulnerably out-of-phase with wider social norms, in their institutionally defined roles.

But anomalies aside, this comparative evidence strongly supports the King and Ripton (1970) interpretation that institutional factors are primary determinants of an instructional environment. Presumably, if teachers had greater control over these factors, their own predominant value orientations would find more expression. However, as Spady (1977) points out, these liberal educational values are systematically undercut by the proliferation of non-educative functions which have been foisted upon public education by a society that sees its schools as the appropriate locus for performing such intrinsically authoritarian functions as social sorting, socialization to work roles, and custodial care. Since these non-educative functions, which demand administrative, as distinct from educative, accountability, become the legal responsibilities of the school and its personnel, they naturally tend to dominate the operational activities of the school staff. The accountability implications of Spady's functional divisions will be examined more thoroughly in the forthcoming section on teacher performance evaluation.

CHARACTERISTIC PROFILE AND TREND SUMMARY

The personal characteristics of Canada's teachers are diverse and complex. They are also undergoing change. It is therefore difficult to project an accurate profile of the 'average teacher.' A perhaps more insightful summarization is achieved through a 'probability' review.

For example, there are now nearly as many male teachers as female – a dramatic equalization from the close to three-to-one female dominance that was characteristic three decades ago. However, if one were to enter a Canadian elementary school classroom today, there is still a two-thirds chance that the teacher would be a woman. At the high-school level, in contrast, males continue to outnumber females in approximately the same two-thirds ratio. The resulting picture is one of significant gender-based segmentation within the overall teaching force. This segmentation borders on discrimination when classroom teaching is separated from teaching positions with added administrative responsibility. The chance of finding a woman occupying either the principal's or vice-principal's office in a Canadian school remained through the mid-1980s historically consistent at one in seven or eight.

Ethnically, nearly 56 per cent of all Canadian teachers come from family backgrounds that originated in the United Kingdom. This is a 12 per cent over-representation in relation to the Anglo population as a whole. The 19 per cent of all teachers who come from French-language origins are under-representative of their population base by 10 per cent. The under-representation of teachers of French-origin would appear to reflect the French-Canadian migration out of Quebec, and perhaps variations in the student-teacher ratios and participation rates in Quebec and the rest of Canada. Those 27 per cent of teachers who come from neither Anglo nor French ethnic origins are proportional to their 'residual' population ratio. However, there is good reason to suspect that certain minorities, such as native Canadians, are seriously under-represented.

In terms of socio-economic origins, both male and female teachers are now recruited from the middle class in about the same proportion – close to 40 per cent. Approximately one-quarter come from upper-class origins and one-third from lower socio-economic backgrounds. This represents a recent shift from the relatively high proportion of males (60 per cent) who were traditionally recruited from lower-status origins.

The probability of finding a teacher under the age of 35 declined during the 1970s from two-out-of-three to less than one-out-of-three. By the 1980s over one-half of all teachers fell into the mid-career range – between 35 and 49 years of age. It will take until almost the year 2010 before the age-distribution peak of in-service teachers reaches the retirement exit point.

A very high proportion of all teachers (85 per cent) have now attained a university degree. This represents a dramatic increase from the one-third proportion of thirty years ago. It is in the elementary division that the qualification improvements have been most dramatic. Since most younger teachers are now graduates, it is anticipated that soon close to 100 per cent of teachers will hold degrees.

The professional training of teachers is characterized by a relatively short program, which perhaps more than most other professional training attempts to balance instrumental and humanistic elements. Historically, the prerequisites, admission, and graduation standards for teacher-training and licensing have not been high. However, admission standards have been recently brought into conformity with other academically based professional schools. Although the professional training year is a universal requirement for licensing, its value, beyond facilitating the role shift from student to teacher, has been a subject of controversy. With respect to the effective socialization to professional norms and practice the instructional component of teacher-training is seen to be weak in comparison with the 'imprint' of the practicum and later institutional practices.

The majority of teachers seem to occupy the ideological middle ground. However, in comparison with the working population as a whole, a higher proportion of teachers hold 'liberal-humanistic' values. Other evidence, however, suggests that organizational imperatives, more than personal values, determine the actual classroom behaviour of teachers.

4

Conditions of Work and Career Patterns

The overwhelming majority of schoolteachers are public employees of local or regional boards of education which function under the legislative aegis of provincial ministries (or departments) of education. While it is the local board that is the direct employer, the provincial ministry is the certifying authority. The usual employment practice for properly certified teachers is a set probationary period followed by the granting of tenure if the probationary teacher's contract is renewed. Tenured teachers cannot be terminated without formal demonstration of cause, or lack of demand for service. Historically, the interpretation of the terms of employment were assumed under the education ministry's administration of provincial public school legislation. However, the contractual terms of teacher employment are increasingly being determined through collective bargaining, either with the local boards individually or through their province-wide bargaining agencies.

SCOPE OF WORK

At the core of teacher's work, of course, is classroom instruction. Most teachers are actively engaged in the classroom or its equivalent for 20 to 25 hours a week. In the early grades, a teacher is responsible for all, or almost all, the subjects the students are taught. Subject specialization becomes more common in the junior and senior secondary divisions. However, even at the most senior levels it is normal for teachers to teach several often quite disparate subjects.

The degree to which subject specialization is recognized as a condition of work varies. Oddly enough, specialization appears to be less well defined at the academic core than at the periphery. Library, vocational, home economics, physical education, art, and life-skill teachers are more likely to teach exclusively or predominantly within the area of their own specialized training than are literature, history, geography, and language teachers. Even science and mathematics teachers are often expected to teach subjects well removed from their own specialty in order to balance timetables. Subject specialization opportunities are naturally greater in larger districts and at secondary levels.

But even where subject specialization is emphasized, the instruction for which schoolteachers are held responsible often goes beyond subject-matter to include behavioural conditioning and attitudinal socialization. In essence, this means ensuring that students conform to those personal and group behaviour standards which have been more or less officially sanctioned as appropriate within the classroom and beyond, to the limits of the school's jurisdiction. Less obvious is the conveying of attitudinal norms that conform to the school's 'sensitivity' to dominant societal values. While some subjects are more and some less sensitive to value interpretation, all teachers are expected to exercise some judgment regarding the balance between conforming and non-conforming world-views.

Since school-sanctioned behaviour norms and value conventions will not always conform closely to those held by students from socially or culturally divergent backgrounds, teachers often experience significant behavioural tensions. Further, teachers are expected to be able to manage all but the most severe of the student/teacher or parent/teacher conflicts that arise. Indeed, one of the most salient criteria upon which official teacher performance evaluation rests is the extent to which such problems are successfully contained within the classroom. Since the teacher controls very few enforcement instruments (those that do exist are vested with higher levels of administrative authority), it matters a great deal how a teacher's own personal characteristics articulate with those that predominate among his or her students and the families and community from which they come.

If a teacher fails to maintain the school's acceptable level of formal classroom order, or must appeal to higher authority to do so, he or she is likely to be viewed by that higher authority as a poor teacher. As a consequence, those teachers who find themselves in antagonistic classroom environments often resort to what one observer has termed a 'negotiated order' (Martin 1976). Within such an order the teacher may be forced to trade off instruction that is not appreciated by the students for the behavioural conformity that is required by the system. Critics have noted that where the norms and values of the school and those possessed by students are sharply divided, this negotiated order leads to a situation where the de facto work of teachers becomes more custodial than educational. All too often this reinforces the social inequalities that produced the student/teacher tensions in the first place.

In addition to classroom activities, teachers must devote time to the preparation of lessons and the evaluation of student work. The evaluation function not only provides students and parents with indications of progress, but also serves as the basis for the sorting of students into various 'streams' which differentiate students in terms of achievement and/or aptitude. Because this sorting has consequences for further educational and occupational opportunities, teachers are actually required to make critical social allocation decisions (Cicourel & Kitsuse 1963). Since this social-agent role has a direct effect on the life-chances of students, teachers are also required to maintain legally defined records and engage in report writing so as to ensure that the decisions that are made are legitimized through formal documentation and administrative review.

Though less contractually specified than the classroom duties, out-of-class and extra-curricular supervision of various kinds is also a work expectation. Staff meetings, parent interviews, and inter-agency consultations are less specified, but often time-consuming, obligations.

Although there has recently been some experimentation with team-teaching and the use of teaching assistants, most of the diverse work expected of teachers continues to be undertaken in collegial isolation and without significant clerical support. The typical absence of any private work space, or even access to a convenient telephone, causes significant problems for teachers. The almost time-clock rigidity of the daily routine, with few if any discretionary periods, also creates personal scheduling problems that would surely be considered unacceptable by most other professional workers.

Finally, teachers are expected to provide positive role models not only within the school but also in the community. While the puritanical behavioural codes that were once strictly imposed upon teachers, especially women teachers, have softened over time, it is still expected that teachers exercise some reasonable decorum with respect to their public persona.

In summary, the work public school teachers do encompasses a broad range of activities with classroom instruction at the core and extra-curricular activities at the periphery. Between lie a number of quasi administrative, public relations, behavioural control, and social agency duties. Although aspects of this work may be discretionary, most of the core work is strongly prescribed in terms of content, form, and timing. Although the work is quite independent in the sense that most classroom instruction occurs without direct supervision or peer involvement, teaching is also vulnerable in the sense that teachers perform before a predominantly non-voluntary, often sceptical, and sometimes outright hostile clientele that may well precipitate the wrath of well-situated parents or powerful community groups should they decide to make trouble. Successful teachers are thus required at one and the same time to be privately resourceful and publicly adroit. If one were to try to define the innate personal qualities that would best serve teachers in performing their work, such qualities as 'perception,' 'judgment,' 'patience,' and perhaps above all, 'empathy' come to mind.

RECRUITMENT AND ATTACHMENT

Lortie (1975) argues the importance of recruitment dynamics when he notes, 'the *way* an occupation fits into the competitive recruitment system will affect its social composition and its inner life ... which ensure an occupation will come to be staffed by people of particular dispositions and life circumstances' (25–6). He goes on to say that the 'ecological process' of recruitment contains both 'attractor' and 'facilitator' mechanisms.

It will be recalled from a previous discussion that the 'blocked aspiration' attractor and the 'easy convertibility' facilitator in teacher recruitment were particularly operant during the period when the surplus of university graduates began to overtake the market for highly qualified personnel. Indeed, by the late 1960s, teaching became the first, though for many not the last, occupational destination for approximately 50 per cent of all university graduates (see Table 3.8). However, it must not be assumed that all those who enter teaching are so superficially motivated. Despite the one-year 'easy convertibility' option, many of those with a clear sense of vocational calling choose to major in pedagogy at the beginning rather than the end of their undergraduate education.

There exists a significant body of research into the occupational motivations of in-service teachers. Lortie (1975) has combined the results of the National Education Association surveys with his own research to provide a comprehensive picture of what attracts American teachers to the classroom. In brief, the motivational pattern of U.S. teachers ranges from altruistic to instrumental. At the altruistic end may be found the desire to work with children and a strong personal service orientation. Instrumental motivations include material benefits, time compatibility, security, social mobility, long vacations, and, as already mentioned, blocked aspirations and easy convertibility. Somewhere between lie such social-psychological factors as identification with a role-model teacher, family influence, labelling by a significant other, and, in the case of the 'dutiful daughter,' compliance with parental restrictions on other kinds of work.

While Lortie rightly warns that there is a considerable variety of motives, his analysis nevertheless leads to the conclusion that

The recruitment system is canted to ... encourage people who have only limited interests in the occupational affairs of teaching. We can see this clearly in the case of time compatibility; one would not expect people who choose teaching because it makes limited demands on their time to invest the effort needed to change either the context or the conduct of classroom teaching ... While early deciders may act conservatively because they are living out identifications with figures from the past, late (usually male) entrants may lack the motivation to challenge historic patterns. Many male teachers, in fact, are upwardly mobile and likely to construe their interests as lying in the administrative domain; they may feel that their personal advancement depends on maintaining a hierarchy. (53, 54)

These last observations bring into sharp relief the relationship between recruitment and job attachment, or the degree to which a field of work retains those who enter it. In general, it has been demonstrated that the more an occupation is selective in its recruitment and offers not only extrinsic rewards but also intrinsic satisfactions and ongoing opportunities for personal development, the greater will be the lifelong occupational commitments of those who are recruited (Hall 1969; Slocum 1966; Taylor 1968). It is, of course, the professional occupations that are assumed to offer the greatest opportunity for this intrinsic satisfaction and ongoing development, and hence it is professionals who should have the highest levels of attachment.

But, as has already been noted, very few occupations in the officially designated 'professional and managerial' category have demonstrated such a low attachment pattern as schoolteaching. The U.S. Office of Education reported in 1967 a national turnover of 8 per cent annually, which amounts to a 50 per cent attrition in ten years. Addington (1965) found that the largest proportion of those who leave do so within three to five years. Although the higher rewards offered in other occupations have been widely assumed as the main reason for leaving, Linderfield's (1961) analysis of causal factors in recruitment and separation found that although remuneration was an important determinant of recruitment, there was little relationship between salary and separation rates. Stinnett's (1969) study of teacher drop-outs identifies dissatisfaction with working conditions and excessive administrative interference as major causes of early leaving.

Although Schlechty and Vance (1981) found that these historically very high separation rates declined somewhat under the worsening labour-market conditions that developed in the late 1970s, they also found that the attrition rates were highest for the most academically able, while retention rates were highest for the least able. Given this and other confirming evidence (e.g., Roth 1983; Feistritzer 1983; Villeme & Hall 1983–4) that attachment and competence are inversely related, Watts (1984) has questioned whether teaching shouldn't be reinstitutionalized as a desirably 'come-and-go profession.'

There has not been as much systematic research in Canada on teacher attachment, but similarly low levels of retention have been widely assumed on the basis of inferential evidence. For example,

Small (1970) found that less than one-quarter of her sample of active Newfoundland teachers were firmly committed to teaching as a career. One-half were openly ambivalent about their commitment to teaching, and one-quarter remained in the role only because they would pay too high a penalty for leaving. Branscombe (1969) offers confirming data for British Columbia, where only 17 per cent of his sample indicated that they planned to continue teaching as a lifelong career. Another 27 per cent indicated that they had definite plans to leave the profession, while 56 per cent indicated that they would 'realistically' continue on as teachers, but would like to pursue other options if and when available. King and Ripton's (1970) sample of secondary school teacher-trainee candidates from Ontario reveals that the relatively low attachment to the teaching profession begins prior to entry. Only 14 per cent of the male and 7 per cent of the female student-teachers expected to be teaching fifteen years after commencing teaching. Although the low percentage of females is, or at least was at the time, likely related to the anticipation of child-rearing, the early classroom departure expectation on the part of 80 per cent of the males was predicated on the presumption that they would end up in an occupation of higher status than that of teaching – 55 per cent in school administration.

Valuable as these local studies are in pointing out teacher attachment trends for Canada, the Highly Qualified Manpower (HQM) survey (1973), jointly conducted for the Secretary of State and Statistics Canada, provides an opportunity to obtain more comprehensive information on Canadian teacher attachment patterns. A special run of this data base was made in which those who indicated teaching as their first full-time occupation were checked to see if they were still employed as teachers at the time of the survey. Controls for age group, sex, and teaching level were also applied.

As Table 4.1 reveals, those who began their teaching careers in the 1950s or earlier (the over-40 group) had the lowest attrition rate, despite the fact that they had the longest time to find alternatives. The middle-tenure group (age 30–39), most of whom would have started their teaching careers between 1955 and 1965, have attachment rates that conform to the high U.S. rates for the same period. However, those Canadian teachers who began their careers in the late 1960s or early 1970s (the under-30 group) show an extraordinarily high rate of attrition that is half again higher than the U.S. rates for the same period. Since this was the period of maximum teaching-force expansion, when temporary teaching permits were easily obtained, it is likely that many of these short-staying individuals simply found teaching a convenient stopgap while planning to continue their education in another field or while awaiting other job openings. Nevertheless, when, by 1973, three-quarters of the male and nearly two-thirds of the female teachers had left for other work in less than ten years, the occupation could only be described as dominated by transients.

Information on which occupations those who leave teaching enter was also obtained from the HQM study. Table 4.2 shows clearly that other professional and managerial employment is over-whelmingly the destination.

Unfortunately there is no data source beyond 1973 that is similarly comprehensive. However, it is likely that the general decline in the market for highly qualified manpower will have reduced the early leaving rates, while the recently imposed higher recruitment standards may well serve to increase the occupational commitment of those who do become teachers.

Of course teaching not only produces 'out-migrants' but also attracts 'in-migrants' from other occupations. The HQM survey provided comparable data on those who are currently teaching but who came from other occupational origins. Table 4.3 shows the distributions, with the same controls applied as in the case of the out-migrants. Although the net exchange is very definitely not in favour of teaching – with out-migration at twice the rate of in-migration – teaching has nevertheless proved an attractive option to many well-qualified individuals who were apparently dissatisfied with their original occupational choices (see Table 4.4). Not surprisingly, those who migrate into teaching have a much higher long-term attachment rate than those who become teachers immediately after completing their own education. Given this, it is unfortunate that this more mature avenue of recruitment has not been as institutionally favoured as the direct-out-of-college route – especially in view of the potential it held for balancing the age compositional distortions that have been already discussed.

While these findings clearly reveal the job attachment patterns of those who start their careers as teachers, they do not include the first level of attrition, i.e., those who complete a teacher-training program and receive certification to enter the profession but fail to exercise this option. The HQM survey data base included information that could be accessed to provide this data.

The pattern of 'no shows,' as seen in Table 4.5, reveals males as less likely to take up teaching after qualification. Indeed, back in the 1940s and early 1950s, over one-half the male qualifiers compared to only one-fifth of the women failed to pursue a teaching career after qualification. For these males, the alternative managerial and professional occupations again proved to be the big attraction. This extraordinarily high rate of male non-entry gradually declined through to the early 1970s, when sexual parity was achieved at just over 70 per cent of the teacher-education graduates of both sexes entering teaching. However, while this is clearly a major overall improvement, it represents a significant increase in 'no show' women, who are now much more prone to follow other occupations than was the case in earlier graduating cohorts. Here again, the historical data reveal that men and women are converging from opposite directions. The decline in alternative professional job openings for men, and the change in occupational aspirations (and opportunities) of women, would seem to be the most plausible explanation.

REMUNERATION

Like most other public service employees, teachers have over the last quarter-century experienced a significant increase in remuneration relative to those in other occupations. Traditionally, it was assumed that the inherent security, gentility, and fringe benefits of public service employment represented a significant offset to a comparatively lower – in some cases much lower – salary scale. However, as the security and benefits practices in the private sector increased, and paternalism in the public service generally decreased, so too did the sanguine acceptance of pay-scale differentials.

In the case of teachers, there were several other factors. Most notably, the rapid expansion period created shortages at a time of generally high demand for workers in the same market sector. This inevitably produced some pay competition. As noted, there was during the post-war decade a general increase in public respect for, and expectations of, education. If, as the first and second *Annual*

Reviews of the Economic Council of Canada (1964/5) argued, education was to be the panacea by which the post-modern state of perfection could be attained, then the spectacle of schoolteachers living a threadbare existence was not ideologically consistent. Finally, the drive to upgrade the academic credentials of in-service as well as new-entrant teachers also legitimized pay-scale advances.

The extent to which these factors served to increase both the actual and the relative income position of teachers is depicted in Table 4.6. Here, the annual median salaries of Canadian schoolteachers are compared with the industrial wage composite between 1955 and 1983 in terms of both current and real dollar values.[1]

As is evident, the 1955 median teaching-force's annual remuneration lagged some 11 per cent behind the industrial composite wage. However, by 1958 teacher salaries had passed the industrial composite and continued to make gains. On average, over the twenty-eight-year period, the increase in teacher remuneration in real dollar values was in the order of three times that of the industrial composite wage over the same period. By comparing the changes in these two remuneration averages, it is apparent that schoolteaching has been moving up in terms of remuneration relative to the industrial worker occupational category. However, the very last 1983 entry suggests that this relative growth may now be ending.

According to Havinghurst's (1958) model of occupational group mobility factors, all of the conditions which tend to promote the fortunes of one occupational group over another were applicable to teachers between 1955 and the mid-1970s. Specifically, 'differential fertility,' 'technological change,' 'social ideology,' and 'general economic expansion' all functioned in a positive direction for teachers. But as Havinghurst's model would also predict, any reversal in these extrinsic factors was bound to foster some negative indicators. Our previous discussions should leave little doubt that by the

---

1 The annual industrial composite wage figures were obtained by multiplying the Statistics Canada annual average weekly wage (SC 11-003) by 52. The inflation control was achieved by recalculating the annual average all-category consumer price index (SC 11-003) between 1955 and 1983 after setting 1971 at 100.

mid-1970s these negative conditions began to prevail. The Table 4.6 remuneration data clearly reflect this decline, though in the case of teachers, with a lag.

While median salary data are a useful comparative measure, it is worth noting that teacher pay-scales are based upon a rigid formula that differentiates on the basis of both the level of post-secondary educational attainment and the years of teaching experience up to a maximum. Administrative allowances are then typically added on to the teacher pay-scale location held by the individual administrator.

It should also be noted that interregional salary differentials are quite significant, though the recent (1982) agreement between five of the provinces and both of the territories to recognize each other's teacher certification should have the effect of reducing interregional pay differentials. Table 4.7 summarizes these regional variations for basic bachelor's level or equivalent teaching-certificate holders.

A measure of the extent to which administrative promotions, on average, represent an increase in remuneration is presented in Table 4.8. But average salaries do not tell the whole story. Recalling that administrative allowances are added onto the teacher pay-scale, it is also important in comparing the salary averages of teachers and administrators to take account of the influence that seniority has upon average administrative pay relative to average teacher pay. In particular, given that administrative promotions do not normally come before considerable classroom experience is gained, it is likely that administrators will, on average, be higher on the scale than teachers. Table 4.8 indicates, for comparison purposes only, what the salary averages of teachers would be if they had the same experience (scale location) as their administrators.

These teacher/school administration 'average' and 'highest maximum' salary comparisons provide an indication of the added rewards available to those who succeed in making the transition to administration. Certainly these differentials are not great for the bottom rungs but become significant at higher levels. But, as will be explored in a later context, perhaps teachers' greatest incentive in seeking administrative promotion is simply to escape the sense of malaise, even failure, that appears to overtake so many classroom teachers, male teachers especially, by mid-career.

Irrespective of whether the remuneration associated with the work teachers do is seen as a 'reward' for the important human services they perform or as 'compensation' for the frustration they experience, the above salary data suggest that the average pay of a public school teacher has, over the past quarter-century, emerged from below the average industrial wage to the point where it is at least commensurate with skilled technical, semi-professional, and even some professional incomes.

In order to verify this, a special run was made of the Carleton University (1983) Canadian Class Structure survey data base. This special run enabled direct comparisons to be made of teachers with 'Managerial and Professional' as well as 'Hourly Paid' employees; it was also possible to show all three occupational categories distributed over their full range, from lowest to highest incomes. Table 4.9 encapsulates the relevant findings.

In comparing the intervals within which the median income for each group falls, it is apparent that teachers not only enjoy the highest median income, but also have the highest proportion of members at the median income level. However, because of the front-loaded pay-scaling, which sees teachers reaching their maximum salary levels within eight to twelve years, these median incomes are also close to the terminal income. Indeed, only 13.6 per cent of all teachers earn incomes above the median interval. The situation for the 'Managerial and Professional' workers is notably different in that twice as many (26.1 per cent) are located within income intervals above the median and nearly 10 per cent earn twice the median (or more) compared with only 1 per cent of teachers whose earnings fall in that elevated range. Clearly, teachers' pay is now *on average* comparatively good. However, a career in teaching does not offer the same opportunity as many other professional and semi-professional occupations to earn well above the average.

While this ceiling on classroom teacher earnings is in one sense restrictive, it should not obscure the positive effect upon lifetime earnings that a front-loaded, in comparison with an end-loaded, pay-scale produces. For example, the end-loaded university faculty pay-scale begins at approximately the same level but takes over twice as long to reach its notably higher maximum. As a consequence, based on scale comparisons the lifetime earnings of the average university faculty member, whose career begins significantly later because of longer educational preparation, would not significantly surpass those of the average teacher. Thus, in terms of narrowly defined 'human capital' (Schultz 1961; Machlup 1962) criteria, the relatively low educational 'investments' made to become a schoolteacher would appear to pay very good dividends.

However, the early-peaking teacher pay-scale has the psychological disadvantage of conveying the message, to those who do not make the transition to the administrative ladder, that they are 'stalled-out' relatively early in their careers. Whether this is a contributing factor to the high propensity for the mid-career 'burn-out' that has been widely associated with schoolteaching has not been clearly established (however see Cunningham 1983; Hiebert & Farber 1984).

Of course in today's society, in which an ever-increasing proportion of spouses work, individual income comparisons may be less relevant than family incomes. The same Carleton University survey also asked its respondents to provide comparable information on their family situation and income.

As Table 4.10 indicates, a higher proportion of teachers are living with a spouse or partner than is the case with the other two occupational categories. Of those who are living with a spouse, a notably greater proportion of teachers have working spouses. It is, therefore, very likely that average family incomes of teachers are even higher in comparison to the other occupational groups than the individual income comparisons. Table 4.11 confirms this. Not only does the interval within which the median family income falls now surpass that of the 'Managerial and Professional' category, the aforementioned ceiling on individual incomes imposed by the teacher pay-scale appears to be much less restrictive with respect to family income comparisons, which reveal close to the same proportion of teachers and manager/professionals falling in the highest income brackets.

Given the very real income gains achieved by Canadian teachers over the past twenty-five years, it is doubtful if teachers are any longer as likely to engage in 'moonlighting' as was once assumed to be the case. While reliable historic data on the extent to which the formerly underpaid teachers sought outside employment during free time are hard to come by, the Carleton University data base provides more recent information on secondary sources of earned income. Table 4.12 provides the essential information.

Thus we see that if teachers ever had a propensity to moonlight in order to achieve the standard of living they desired, they are no longer so inclined. Indeed, of the three occupational categories, teachers have the lowest proportion, just 7.3 per cent, though the highest number of hours, 19 per week, devoted to secondary sources of earned income. But there is only a marginal difference among the three occupational categories in their propensity to, or the amount of time devoted to, such supplementary work. There is, however, a curiously substantial difference between teachers and the other occupational categories when it comes to the proportion of those who do seek outside earnings who choose self-employed means. It would seem that teachers either have a low aptitude for self-employment or that their primary employment effectively insulates them from entrepreneurial opportunities.

Finally, it is apparent, from the average time each occupational group reported that they spent pursuing their primary employment, that teachers do not significantly differ from either the 'Managers and Professionals' or the 'Hourly Employed' workers. Again, if teachers were once required to work long hours preparing lessons, grading papers, and supervising extra-curricular activities, the contemporary teacher is not, on average, burdened beyond the working time norms associated with other occupations.

Whether the remuneration gains, in either absolute or relative terms, that have been achieved by teachers can be maintained in a period when the ambient economic and social factors are not as propitious as in the past is questionable. But it is very unlikely that the remuneration teachers receive will ever again descend to the low ebbs of the past. It will also be interesting to see if the rigid pay formulas, which lock the good, the bad, and the indifferent into the same reward system, will be maintained at a time when quality is being promoted over quantity and when public sector accountability is being vigorously pursued at the highest policy levels.

PERFORMANCE EVALUATION

In purely formalistic terms, public schools and those who teach in them are accountable to their provincial legislatures through the minister of education. In practice, direct responsibility for school standards and teacher performance is administered by the provincial ministries of education. These central bureaucracies control the licensing and inspection of schools and teachers through district superintendents (or inspectors). In addition to observing the teacher performing classroom duties, the superintendent examines class attendance records and teaching outlines to ensure conformity with legal and administrative requisites; evaluates classroom cosmetics; and discusses a teacher's performance with the principal and any others, such as the growing number of board 'consultants,' who interact with the teacher in relation to classroom duties.

Teacher reaction to this evaluation procedure tends more toward the cynical than the fearful. The reasons are not hard to find. Superintendents have many other duties and hence do not have the opportunity to inspect an individual teacher very thoroughly. Such brief and irregular visitations which focus on superficials have very little potential for the proper assessment of the open-ended educative functions, as distinct from the prescribed classroom organization and control functions. All concerned understand that the presence of the inspector in the classroom may well distort the normal situation. Standardized measurements are not normally favoured, and the subjective preferences of senior superintendents become common staff-room knowledge which may be utilized cynically during the brief visitation. Finally, with the exception of extreme cases, inspector's reports tend toward a cautiously 'satisfactory' rating, which neither praises good work nor damns poor performance.

Given these characteristics of the formal departmental-level teacher evaluation procedure, it is not surprising that whenever information on the professional competency of a teacher is required (e.g., when transfer to another school or district is requested), considerable use is made of the informal administration information network. In either the formal or informal networks, it is reasonable to assume, given the priorities of those who do the evaluating, that administrative criteria would typically outweigh educational criteria. In this regard it is interesting to compare school-teacher evaluation to university faculty evaluation procedures. The latter, which in most respects cleave much closer to the professional model, are based upon collegial evaluations that involve external peer reviews.

But even if the hierarchical evaluation model is accepted as appropriate in the public school context, it is noteworthy that the criteria of competency have not been very clearly delineated. This reluctance to utilize systematic evaluation criteria is all the more surprising given the extensive research that has gone into the determination of which teacher performance characteristics are most associated with student achievement (e.g., Hamachek 1969; Knoop 1980; Valdes 1982).

Among the most rigorous and revealing of the research into the characteristics of the successful teacher is that conducted by the American Council of Education (Ryans 1960). This seminal study was among the first to apply advanced social-scientific measurement and analysis techniques to the determination of those teacher characteristics which are associated with higher and lower levels of student motivation and performance. In essence this study revealed that those teachers who maintained higher levels of outside interests were more successful than those who did not. Teachers with higher levels of academic achievement were notably more effective than those with lower achievement records. Individuals with well-established humanistic values and strong public-service motivations were more successful than those with predominantly authoritarian values and instrumental motivations. Teachers from both the highest and lowest socio-economic backgrounds had better success than those from the middle levels. Clearly, such findings raise important questions with respect to established teacher-recruitment, training, and reward practices.

While no definitive answers to such troublesome questions are readily available, a number of plausible inferences may be drawn from evidence already discussed. For example, it will be recalled from King and Ripton's (1970) study of Ontario secondary school teachers that when teachers were asked to delineate the perceived performance characteristics that were most associated with effective teaching and those required for moving up to administrative positions, the 'ability to transfer knowledge' fell from first to fifth place. This is hardly surprising, given that the school administration's performance is measured primarily in terms of their capacity to ensure social control and perform prescribed bureaucratic functions.

Thus any formal teacher-evaluation procedure that is administration rather than peer dominated is likely to reflect management imperatives in the not unrealistic expectation that teachers will take these managerial imperatives seriously enough not to challenge them in their pursuit of educative goals. The contradictory effect of this arrangement is well encapsulated in the cynical apho-

rism regularly overheard in school staff-rooms: 'what is educationally desirable is administratively impossible.' Nevertheless, the
tactic is well rooted in the managerial theorem that argues the
most effective way to achieve worker compliance is through the
criteria of performance evaluation. This is the case especially if
there is a disjunction between an organization's rhetorical and
operational priorities. Those who seek advancement tend to tune
their sensitivities to the operational priorities latent within the
evaluation criteria.

But having noted this, it is only fair to note that the bureaucratic bias in teacher evaluation is not just the product of administrative expediency. These same administrators are aware, often pain-
fully so, that public expectations of schooling include agendas that
have nothing to do with the educative function. In this regard,
Spady (1977) identifies 'five major functions that public schools in
North America are expected to perform in dealing with their students' (360). These are: 'instruction, socialization, custody-control,
evaluation-certification and selection' (360). Spady then argues
from solid evidence that for the instructional role to be properly
fulfilled, the teacher must rely heavily upon the voluntary compliance and involvement of the student within an empathic pedagogic climate. Since client voluntarism and practitioner empathy
are held to be the essential prerequisites of any professional relationship, the educative role is clearly a professional one. Like all
such professional roles, the educative function requires the teacher
to give priority to the student's needs over and above any outside
interest agendas. However, the other functions that Spady identifies as part of the public education package place the teacher in
the role of 'agent' for just such outside-interest intervention. It is in
the performance of their duties as agents that teachers find it
necessary to set aside their role as professionals in order to fulfil
various bureaucratically prescribed functions.

Clearly this represents a serious role-conflict for the teacher,
especially when it is realized that the intellectual, developmental
goal of instruction is to broaden the perceptions and responses of
students, whereas the other functions all seek to limit student
perceptions and responses. As Spady puts it: 'The paradox is that
the more effective the school [teacher] is as an agent of instruction,
the more capable students will be of seeking sources of information
and capitalizing on experiences that further expand their horizons

and make them aware of potentially available alternatives. This growing awareness stands in sharp contrast to control mechanisms, systems of rules, and socialization strategies that attempt to narrow or restrict access to ideas, information, settings or experiences' (367).

If this interpretation is correct (cf. Regan's 1977 thesis on classroom socialization biases) then there is at least some basis for presuming that the support for teacher-evaluation procedures that undercut the teacher's professional educative role goes well beyond the narrowly defined interests of school administrators – some of whom, despite the selection bias, strive to minimize the negative impact of bureaucratic ritualism on their teaching staff.

In any event, so long as the several functions of public education remain ambiguous and contradictory, and so long as teacher evaluation procedures fail to reward those teachers who get *educative* results over those who focus on *control* functions, the teaching career system is likely to continue to engender a high level of cynicism.

AUTONOMY AND CONTROL

In order to get a more precise understanding of the relative degree of work autonomy and control which Canadian teachers actually enjoy relative to their aspirations, Carleton University's Canadian Class Structure Survey (1983) data base was again subjected to a special run. Respondents were asked to make 'is' versus 'ought' distinctions, i.e., to indicate specifically 'how much influence each of the groups listed has on what happens in the place where you work' (Q. 85a), followed by 'If it were up to you, how much influence do you think each of these groups *ought* to have ...' (Q. 85b). The 'groups listed' were: 'Managers,' 'The employees as a group,' 'Employee or union representatives (if applicable),' and 'You personally.'

Obviously, the professional-autonomy norms would be reflected in responses that identified high influence at the individual and/or co-worker (collegial) group levels. Alternatively, low professional-autonomy norms would be clearly reflected if high levels of influence were associated with either the managerial or union level.

The percentage of positive answer distributions is displayed in Table 4.13. With regard to the 'reality' answer distribution, teachers attribute a very high level of influence over the work they do to their 'managers' (77.5 per cent) and a very low level to either themselves as individuals (15.2 per cent) or as a collegial group (27.5 per cent). Their union (20.8 per cent) is not appraised as having much influence on decision-making.

With regard to the 'preferred' situation, the teachers do not appear to be exceptionally committed to full professional autonomy. While they would like to see a more equitable sharing of influence between their administrators (58.4 per cent) and the collegial group (54.0 per cent), their desire to have more individual autonomy, although twice that of the 'reality' assessments, was still surprisingly low (31.6 per cent).

In comparing the is/ought discrepancies of teachers to those of the three other occupational categories, it is apparent that teachers come much closer to hourly paid employees than to the managerial and professional group. This is a pattern that will be examined more closely in the 'Satisfactions and Dissatisfactions' discussion.

Given the contradictory evidence that teachers strongly desire professional *recognition*, but have somewhat restricted aspirations for professional *autonomy*, it may be useful to examine more closely just how teachers view the boundaries of their professional responsibilities as distinct from their status aspirations.

In one exceptionally revealing study of teachers in fourteen urban Alberta schools, Simpkins and Friesen (1969) compared the teachers' actual and preferred participation in their school's various decision-making processes. By dividing these processes into the *classroom* locus of 'individual teacher' decisions, the *collegial* locus of the 'staff group,' and the *bureaucratic* locus of the 'higher official authority,' it was discovered that teachers were quite satisfied with their autonomy at the individual classroom level, but highly dissatisfied with their autonomy at the collegial level because of the dominance of the bureaucratic level in all matters outside the classroom. However, the study revealed one crucial exception to the dissatisfaction with bureaucratic officialdom's monopoly on higher-level decision-making. 'Teachers preferred those in higher official authority to play the major role in deciding questions concerned with the basic outline of the curriculum' (14).

Given that the 'special knowledge' upon which teachers' claims to professional status are predicated is significantly oriented to curricular planning and delivery skills, this is contradictory evidence indeed. The point was not lost on the study's authors, who conclude with the following assessment of teachers' commitment to professionalism:

[A] higher degree of professionalization of the teacher's role was reflected in teacher preferences than in teacher perceptions of what actually exists. The major decision-making authority of the teacher was seen to be limited to the immediate work setting of the classroom. However, teachers expressed a desire to extend the decision-making authority to matters of administrative concern. In important respects, teachers preferred an authority structure characteristic of the full-fledged professional organization.

However, unqualified teacher support for the full-fledged professional ideology was not apparent in this study. Teachers preferred to have those in higher official authority continue to exercise major decision-making authority in determining the basic outline of the curriculum. Thus, in a task activity central to the definition of basic school *goals* and *means*, teachers were content to see those in administrative positions exercise major decision-making authority. (15, 16, emphasis added)

Once again, we are reminded of both Johnson's (1972) distinction between 'collegiate' and 'mediative' levels of professionalization and Derber's (1983) distinction between autonomous 'means' and autonomous 'goals.' In the traditional concept of 'collegiate'-based professionalism, control of both the means and goals of the professional activity is maintained. Derber argues that in the more 'mediative' environment of the employed knowledge worker, it is possible for such workers to maintain control over all or some of the means, but not the ends. It would seem that public school teachers in Canada succeed in maintaining some significant autonomy with respect to their 'classroom management' roles. But beyond this obviously constrained boundary, not only the reality but also the expectation of professional control becomes assimilated within the complex organizational system of bureaucratic control.

SATISFACTIONS AND DISSATISFACTIONS

The concept of 'alienation' focuses attention on the degree of worker dissatisfaction which arises from the loss of control over the work process (Friedmann 1955). The growth of alienation, and the social pathologies that attend it, are widely attributed to bureaucratic management's propensity to limit the opportunities for employed workers to engage in self-direction and innovation (Braverman 1974; Rinehart 1975). As noted in Chapter One, 'professionalization' has been identified as the process by which knowledge-based occupations seek to exempt themselves from these alienating trends; and 'deprofessionalization' is the process by which the forces of centralized control seek to appropriate the self-management principles of established professional occupations.

In the above discussion of autonomy and control, evidence was presented which indicated that teachers maintain significant levels of professional autonomy in the administration of the classroom but have little control over the administrative or policy environment within which these classroom activities are located. Given this, the question of how teachers *subjectively* interpret the fundamentally contradictory 'professional' versus 'bureaucratic' systems of control that coexist within their career system becomes the key to determining their net level of satisfaction. In essence, it is the perceived disjunction between expectation and experienced reality that is crucial to any evaluation of work satisfaction.

Certainly there is no shortage of studies on this subject. Indeed, the persistent interest in teacher-satisfaction research over the years hints strongly of the lack of attention to their virtually universal findings. The following examples are representative of the vast literature on the subject. In a national sample of Canadian teachers, Francoeur (1963) found that exclusion from participation in policy-making contributed significantly to teacher dissatisfaction. Pallenson (1970) discovered that the opportunity to employ preferred teaching methods and content significantly contributed to teacher satisfaction. In Schmit's (1968) study of teachers from thirty-three Canadian schools, it was revealed that satisfaction with the school organization is inversely related to the level of perceived bureaucratization.

This finding was confirmed by Gosin's (1970) investigation of female teachers in Ottawa. Comparing the satisfaction levels of teachers with personality types that reflect various degrees of need for 'order,' it was found that while schools that exhibited higher levels of bureaucratic control produced a much lower level of overall satisfaction, 'order-seeking' teachers were more satisfied than those with less need for order. This suggests that, assuming the availability of teacher transfers between schools, there may be a self-allocating principle at work that ensures the matching of liberal versus authoritarian personality types with schools which have similarly polarized administrative philosophies.

Bourne's (1970) study of teacher satisfaction variables in twenty Toronto schools serving neighbourhoods of differing socio-economic status adds yet another dimension to such a distribution by observing that teachers in higher social-status neighbourhoods derive satisfactions from such 'job context' items as administrative style, colleagues, and students; whereas those teaching in lower social-status neighbourhoods derive satisfactions from such 'job content' items as curriculum, teaching aids, and other school facilities. These and other findings (e.g., Nordstrom, Friedenberg & Gold 1967) strongly suggest that the 'liberal and humanistic' versus 'instrumental and authoritarian' division in teacher values may be selectively distributed according to the predominant social values found within the neighbourhood that any particular school serves (c.f. Johnson 1968).

Pelton's (1977) study of the ambiguities associated with the teacher-counsellor role is also revealing of the professional versus bureaucratic tensions that may produce staff conflict. It was found that in schools where the administration respected the professional-counselling principles of client confidentiality and unmediated relations, there was a high level of satisfaction. But where 'non-guidance-oriented principals viewed guidance personnel as having no legitimate professional function and saw them merely as extra hands to be used at the "whim" of the principal,' there was a high potential for 'intrarole conflict' (380).

Allen, Hamelin, and Nixon (1976), in a study of nineteen Greater Vancouver schools, found more dissatisfaction among teachers in open-area classroom settings than in more conventional settings. But these same teachers reported higher satisfaction when teaching open-ended rather than highly prescribed curricula. When controlled for 'personality type,' the satisfaction level was highest for the combination of closed classroom and open curriculum among teachers who had the least need for structure. While the congruence between a preference for open curriculum and closed classrooms appears at first glance anomalous, it will be recalled that Simpkins and Friesen (1969) found that teachers perceived that their professional prerogatives essentially ended beyond the (presumably closed) classroom door. Certainly the open-classroom concept does threaten the privileged and private relationship with the client that is much valued by all who identify with professional norms.

This threat to professional norms was specifically identified by Arikado (1977) as the principal reason for dissatisfaction with team-teaching. By having an officially designated team leader, and dividing the teaching labour between a number of individuals, the professional preference for non-differentiated status relations with colleagues was being undermined.

Although not directly comparable, the evaluation by Fullan, Eastabrook, and Biss (1977) of an experiment in equalitarian involvements by teachers and students in structural and curricular change reinforces Arikado's conclusion that it is not the sharing of responsibilities with others so much as the imposed hierarchy of authority relationships that produces the teacher dissatisfaction.

In a major Alberta study of teacher satisfaction, Holdaway (1978) found that working with students and peer relations produced satisfaction for teachers, while community interference, school administrative practices, departmental policies, physical conditions, student attitudes, and salary levels all produced dissatisfaction. Again, it is significant that the elements that produce the satisfactions are closely associated with professional traits, whereas those that produced dissatisfactions derive from bureaucratic processes.

While these local studies provide a great deal of understanding of the sources and extent of dissatisfaction experienced by teachers with differing personal characteristics over specific features of the work environment, they do not provide any systematic basis for determining the extent to which this dissatisfaction differs from that of other occupational groups.

In order to achieve this comparative understanding, the results from a set of questions included in the Carleton (1983) national survey, which had been specifically designed to measure perception of worker-control factors, was examined. The key questions were:

1 Is yours a job in which you *are required* to design important aspects of your own work and to put your ideas into practice?

2 Is it sometimes possible for you to put some of your own ideas into practice, that is, to plan or design some aspect of your own or other people's work?

3 Here are a number of different work activities. For each one, please indicate if you can do this on your job, either officially or unofficially?

a) Decide when to come to work and when to leave work.

b) Take a day off from work without losing pay or having to claim vacation time, sick leave, or put in time later.

c) Considerably slow down your pace of work for a day when you want to.

d) Decide on your own to introduce a new task or work assignment that you will do on your job.

e) Decide on your own *how* to go about doing your job.

4 Do you have a supervisor who is responsible for directing you in your work?

5 Do you have a supervisor to whom you are required to report?

As in the other special runs done on this data base, teachers were separated out from the total employee sample and then compared to all other employees in the 'Managerial and Professional' category as well as to 'Hourly Employees.'[2] The results, which are displayed in Table 4.14, reveal that teachers evaluate as highly present both the 'necessity' and the 'opportunity' to be innovative in the 'design' of their primary classroom duties. In these categories they are close to unanimous, and rank nine to ten points above the positive response rate of other managerial and professional workers. Teachers also lead, though by less than two points, in their satisfaction with the opportunities to decide on how to do their primary work. But in the other six areas of work autonomy, teachers fall significantly, and in some cases dramatically, behind the other 'Managerial and Professional' workers. This is particularly noticeable in the 'work scheduling' and 'introduction of new tasks' (job enlargement) areas where curricular, even extra-curricular, activity falls within the control jurisdiction of higher authority. Teachers also evaluated very negatively their opportuni-

2 It should be noted also that in order to keep all the 'yes' answers consistent with positive 'satisfaction' interpretations, questions 4 and 5 above were reworded in the negative from the original survey's positive form and then assigned the value of 100 – original frequencies.

ties to manage personal time in ways that permit flexibility within and between work and non-work activities. Indeed, on four out of the nine items, the proportion of negative responses was greater than that of hourly employed workers.

While it must be re-emphasized that these subjective evaluations should not be interpreted as a measure of the alienating conditions *objectively* present within each category, the data set does provide a relative measure of the subjectively perceived self-fulfilment opportunities and limitations associated with each occupational group.

Such a comparison not only places in stark relief the extent of overall teacher dissatisfaction, which comes closer to the average for hourly employees than to the average for other highly qualified manpower, but reveals the extent to which the objective evidence of conflicting 'professional' and 'bureaucratic' authority structures is subjectively experienced. On the positive side, teachers both require and are afforded the freedom to be innovative in the way they approach their classroom work. But on the negative side, they are not given commensurate freedom over curricular content and scheduling. Nor are they afforded anywhere near the degree of trust in the form of freedom from direct supervision and reporting – or even the courtesy of control over their own time budgets – that is commensurate with their responsibilities as they see them.

Given the manifest nature of these contradictions, it is hardly surprising that teacher dissatisfaction is rampant, leading to the high rates already noted of early separation among those who are apparently most temperamentally suited and academically prepared. Indeed, it would be hard to imagine an occupational environment that was better designed to feed the indignation and resentment of those who are anxious to assume their full professional responsibility – or one that better provides cynical excuses for those who wish to minimize such responsibilities.

STATUS ATTAINMENT AND COMMUNITY RELATIONS

It will be recalled from discussions in Chapter Three that male teachers historically were recruited from below average socio-economic status (SES) origins, while female teachers tended to come from above average SES backgrounds. More recent evidence, however, indicated that both male and female recruitment was shifting toward the middle SES range. It was then suggested that the long-standing intergenerational mobility pattern – upwards for men and downwards for women – was diminishing. However, for this conclusion to be confirmed, it is necessary to know exactly where schoolteaching is located within some reliable occupational status scale.

A number of occupational ranking scales have been devised, and several are in wide use as comparative instruments. In general, these scales fall into one of two measurement categories. The objective-criteria scales rank occupations according to some quantifiably measurable characteristics such as educational and income attainments. The subjective criteria scales seek a public evaluation of the prestige rankings of a representative range of occupations.

Theoretical fine points aside, the analytic value in comparing a given occupation's rank location on each scale lies in the degree to which the objectively measurable 'achieved' rewards associated with an occupation are commensurate with the subjective status values that are 'ascribed' to the incumbents of that same occupation by the society at large. In general, a high level of congruence has been demonstrated between the two kinds of scales. For example, in Canada, the Blishen Scale (Blishen 1958) has become the predominant objective measure, while the Pineo-Porter (1967) scale is the most widely used subjective scale. In comparing these two scales, Pineo and Porter found overall correlations between their subjective and Blishen's objective measures falling between a low of .88 among the most poorly matched occupational categories to a high of .93 among the most closely matched groupings. By any standards, this is a high level of overall congruence. However, certain individual occupations showed an exceptional degree of disjunction between the materially 'achieved' and socially 'ascribed' status criteria. Schoolteachers were among these anomalies.

Whereas schoolteachers ranked within the first decile (24th out of 320 occupations) on the objective Blishen scale, on the Pineo-Porter socially ascribed scale, teachers fell into the second decile (37th out of 204 occupations).[3] Thus, in terms of their educational and income attainments, the status location of Canadian teachers falls well within the professional occupational range. However, in

3 This was the average of the slightly separated elementary and secondary locations.

terms of public status recognition, teachers find themselves barely at the semi-professional status level.

Similar comparisons of teachers in the United States reveal an even higher degree of divergence between achieved and ascribed status measures. In commenting on this status inconsistency, Havighurst and Levine (1979) conclude that the popular image of the schoolteacher, 'when judged in terms of level of education required, or in terms of income earned ... does not compare favorably with other occupations ... [T]he society may be said to hold an image of the teacher that is not commensurate with teachers' claims to full professional status and recognition' (533).

In an Alberta study, Mackie (1972) attempted to isolate the source of this discrepancy. She found that the 'public image' of the teacher includes such positive attributes as hard work, circumspection, compassion, and dedication, while the negative attributes tended to be associated with the social control aspects of the teacher/student relationship – a finding that echoes Spady's (1977) concerns over the damage done to the (professional) 'empathic' role requirements of instruction by the (bureaucratic) 'authority' role requirements of the socialization, custodial, and sorting functions.

There are undoubtedly other more subtle sources of influence. For example, Johnson (1972) notes that the ascribed status of any professional group tends to be closely associated with either the prestige of the social class from which members are predominantly recruited or the status of their clients. Colombotos (1963) argues that professionalization is also retarded in those occupations that include a significant proportion of women. If this vicarious 'status by association' is indeed a factor, then an occupation that recruits more women than men, but with the men coming from below the median SES family origins, and that caters to a segment of the population that has yet to establish any power or status of its own might well be affected adversely.

However, recent trends would appear to favour a more positive public image. There are now nearly as many male as female teachers. Also, women are entering the more established professions in greater numbers. These factors could contribute to improved public perceptions of teachers. Just how the upward social recruitment trend for males and downward trend for females will be interpreted is hard to assess. But the status-by-association factors are not the only, and perhaps not the most important, factors in establishing professional claims.

Henchey (1977) identifies a more fundamental source of status deprivation. Specifically, the very 'derived' knowledge base upon which teachers seek to lay their claim to professional status is too 'common' to attract much prestige. There is a tragic irony in this since it is precisely the schoolteacher's task to convey the fundamentals rather than the esoterics of knowledge. As a consequence teachers may only claim 'teaching methods' as their unique 'science.' But even this claim is undercut by other professionals which tend to monopolize the production and distribution of the often superficial and certainly faddish curriculum theory and teaching technology. Given the North American practice (notably different from European traditions) of excluding teachers from any significant involvement in the development of the knowledge they purvey, it is hard for them to counter the public image that in its most extreme and cruel form is encapsulated in the jingo, 'Those who can, do. Those who can't, teach. Those who can't teach, teach teachers.'

Certainly, schoolteachers often find themselves intellectually ill-prepared to advance any claims of special knowledge in relation to the population at large. As Marcus (1973) notes, teachers must 'educate students who have easy access to mass media as well as exposure to and training by relatively well-educated parents. Teachers must also learn to utilize equipment designed to incorporate new learning theories. The latter made the teacher vulnerable to accept university and commercial innovations which compete with their own skills' (199).

Unfortunately, ironic causes have a way of spawning ironically self-defeating responses. It may well be that a source of the relatively low prestige ratings of teachers may derive from their attempts to resist outside interference in the professional-client relationship in order to assert their autonomy. To the extent that the teacher's clients are children with concerned parents, some of whom understand well enough the potential effect of teachers' decisions on their children's future opportunities, the teacher may find in the intruding parent not only a pedagogic competitor, sometimes with more subject knowledge, but also an interfering 'lay person,' sometimes with more political power. Not surprisingly, the teacher's gut reaction is to build stone walls. Indeed, the 'what's wrong with our schools' literature is rife with accounts of the school's efforts to keep the parent and the community out, except on terms that are institutionally prescribed and controlled (Edwards 1965; Stamp 1975).

But the effectiveness of this stonewalling is itself dependent upon the very status ascriptions that have not been too generously bestowed upon teachers. The effects of differential status on teacher-parent interaction have formed the subject of research in both small town (e.g., Hollingshead 1949) and large city (e.g., Becker 1953) contexts. These pioneering studies reveal that although teachers tend to resent all parental interference, they submit to those interventions that originate with parents whose status is higher than their own and succeed in warding off parents with lower status.

Given teachers' lack of opportunity for meaningful involvement in administrative and curricular policy, it is not surprising that they jealously guard their control over the classroom settings. But, of course, it is the classroom that is also the school system's most vulnerable point of contact with the community. And if the teachers feel that they have little effective communication with their administrators on policy and program matters, the findings of Lucas and Lusthaus (1977) reveal that the public feels it has even less. Thus school-community conflict tends to centre on the teacher, who may or may not be blameworthy, but in any case has few political or administrative resources to resolve any of the system's larger public-relations problems.

By all informed accounts (Cole 1969; Marcus 1973; Mayer 1969), this fear of community intervention was the motivation behind the unprecedented and unanticipated 'birthplace of teacher unionism' that took place in New York City in 1968. As Marcus (1973) put it:

Civil rights groups began to demand control over the local schools, pressuring for community determination of teacher hiring and firing, administrator responsibility, curricula development etc. Thus, it was ironic that the vanguard of the teacher movement became the first to strike for professional control while under attack from a newly awakened deprived community ... Contracts, then, have become defensive tools, protecting teachers, stabilizing their jobs, *but not advancing their profession*. The clauses specify what teachers will not do, while little is said about what they will do. (208–10, emphasis added)

Thus, in the absence of a professional power base of their own, and in the presence of some real concerns over who might be scapegoated as a result of public disenchantment over public education policies and practices, teachers turned to the very instrument which they had for so long explicitly rejected – collective bargaining.

5

Teacher Associations

The door was opened for the establishment of teacher associations when Egerton Ryerson's plans for public school reform were embodied in the Ontario Common School Act of 1846 – an act which eventually became the model for all other jurisdictions (Johnson 1968). Although it was recognized that the transformation of the dilettante teaching-force of the pre-Ryerson era into a specially trained and licensed body would inevitably be slow, 'the governing ideology' of the first teacher associations was, as Brimer (1985) notes, 'that of professionalism' (5).

However, frustration came early and remained until late. Successive shifts in the demand for teachers, caused by wars, depressions, and changing priorities in public policy, resulted in education ministries overriding the efforts of teacher associations to raise qualification standards and tighten licensing practices (Lutz 1972). Nevertheless, teacher associations succeeded in getting such official recognition as compulsory membership and a consultative role in matters directly affecting working conditions. Although only a pale reflection of the fully professionalized group of teachers Ryerson envisioned, these associations continued to cling to the professional image from their inception in the 1880s until the 1960s, when some quite unanticipated events overtook them.

FROM CONSULTATION TO CONFRONTATION

To say that North American teacher associations underwent a profound change in the 1960s and 1970s would be a gross understatement. Cole's (1969) account of the unprecedented speed with which American teachers abandoned the genteel professionalism of the National Education Association for the militant unionism of the CIO-affiliated American Federation of Teachers identifies the following factors as motives:

- A rapid increase in the relative deprivation experienced by teachers because of the cumulative failure of pay-scales to keep pace with inflation.
- Reduction in the historic salary differential between primary and secondary level teachers, which was seen by the secondary teachers as undermining their prestige.
- Changes in school size and administrative organization, which made the performance of classroom disciplinary functions increasingly difficult.
- Frustration over the lack of professional authority, particularly to the extent that this made teachers vulnerable in the growing conflict between the community and the school.

While this embracing of union militancy by teachers was indeed a radical departure from their long-established image as 'the most conservative, fearful, quiescent, submissive, and docile [of] all professionals' (Marcus 1973:192), there is little in Cole's analysis to suggest that the move to a collective bargaining tactic in any way reflected an abandonment of the fundamentally conservative values that lie at the root of all claims to professional privilege and status. Thus, Marcus's (1973) widely quoted article, in which he brands American teachers as 'militant conservatives,' emphasizes the extent to which the tactical shift from consultation to confrontation was conceived in desperation and nurtured by its early success.

In Canada it was less a competition between old associations and new unions than a transformation of the former into the latter. Nevertheless, the causes have been widely identified in similar terms (Bruno & Nelken 1975; Cole 1969; Fox & Wince 1976; Falk et al. 1982; Fris 1976; Hellriegel et al. 1970; Hennessy 1975;

Radecki & Evans 1980; Selinger 1980). Selinger and Goldhammer (1972) point out that

by 1967 over half of the employed teachers had five years' experience or less. In the same period of time, the proportion of males entering teaching steadily increased ... [and] the level of teacher dissatisfaction with salaries and working conditions also rose ... The inconsistency between their [the teachers'] expertise and responsibility on the one hand, and the locus of authority on the other, is largely what generates the frustration that results in militancy ... [As a consequence] the past few years have seen tense confrontations between boards and teachers in Canada. Most known sanctions have been applied by teachers in efforts to gain their will: black-listing, pink-sheeting, coincidental resignations, work to rule, study sessions, in-dispute listings, protest marches, sponsored public meetings, political action, emergency meetings, and strikes. School boards have taken countervailing action to resist the growing power of teachers. (47–8)

But while Canadian teachers were being rapidly transformed into a more sophisticated 'cosmopolitan' self-interest group (Bayne 1969; Branscombe 1969; Greffen 1969), their school-board employers remained predominantly 'local' in their perception of educational goals and isolated in terms of their organizational tactics (Cistone 1972; Holdaway 1970; Kratzmann 1974; Myhre 1971). In this regard, Lutz (1972) found it 'particularly interesting that no school board seems to learn much from the experience of others ... Each school board alone and school boards collectively apparently believe, first, that the problem [of militant teachers] will never happen to them; next, that if they get tough they will regain or retain their former power; and finally, that because they have lost some power they are totally powerless' (54).

Thus the most immediately apparent effect of this organizational shift by teachers from consultation to confrontation was to diminish the power of local boards and to increase the power of both the teacher associations and the provincial education departments (Bargen 1972; Wiles & Williams 1972). The longer term impact of this reallocation of power on the educational system as a whole will be considered in a later context, but so far as achieving immediate economic benefits is concerned, the confrontation tactic was unquestionably successful (Muir 1970).

UNIONIZATION AND PROFESSIONALIZATION

While the unprecedented adoption of union tactics accurately reflects the growth in material concerns on the part of a youthful membership with rising economic expectations, there can be little doubt that the old concern for attaining professional recognition remained strong and, as a consequence, became a stated negotiation goal within the new collective bargaining process. However, Johnson's (1971) study of the actual performance of collective bargaining by teachers in Alberta reveals that salary and related issues dominated, while issues involving working conditions were essentially omitted from the bargaining table.

Similarly, Harp and Betcherman (1980) in their study of the Ontario Secondary School Teachers Federation found the 'economism' goal to be more prevalent than the professional 'control' goal.

In his comprehensive analysis of collective agreements in all provinces, Marcotte (1984) noted that 'job security' and 'salary' items continued to preoccupy the negotiation agendas of most provincial teachers' associations. Indeed, it was only in British Columbia, Alberta, Saskatchewan, and New Brunswick that any significant attempts to include 'working conditions' were discovered. However, Marcotte, over the three-year period between 1981 and 1984, did not find these isolated attempts to be very successful: 'Our examination of contracts ... demonstrates that teachers in Western Canada have made only a few isolated inroads toward stipulation of working conditions in their collective agreements' (57). On the basis of this survey, Marcotte was able to conclude that there is little evidence that public education 'employer groups ... were losing control of the education service to teachers' (56).

Since Marcotte's survey tends to be rather coarsely tuned to the professional issues and not sufficiently longitudinal to identify emerging trends, Brimer (1985) undertook, especially for this study, a content analysis of a sampling of Ontario collective agreements signed in 1975–6 and again in 1984–5. While less inclusive than the Marcotte study, it provides greater detail over a longer period.

As with any content analysis, the definition of categories is important. After reviewing similar studies relating to other professional unions (Kleingartner & Bickner 1977; Ponak 1981) Brimer established three areas of collective agreement content. Level I items reflect those areas of agreement that are narrowly economic: salary, fringe benefits, retirement benefits, surplus/redundancy provisions, etc. Level II goals reflect items of professional concern but not of professional control: sabbatical or professional-training leave provisions, in-service professional development opportunities, and recognition of higher levels of professional qualifications. Level III items reflect agreements that would ensure at least a sharing of control between the administration and teachers in areas of professional judgment – class size, pupil-teacher ratio, curriculum development – and in other broader areas of educational policy. Finally, so as to identify any counter-trends to the Level III professional control items, Brimer also tabulated evidence of 'management rights' clauses that appeared in the formal contract. While the detailed results are too extensive for presentation here, Brimer's summary conclusions show a clear pattern of priorities emerging over the nine-year span of union/board agreements in Ontario.

With respect to narrowly economic Level I issues, Brimer found that salary increases have been very substantial over the nine-year interval. This increase – of approximately 50 per cent (current dollar values) – was essentially uniform across the elementary and secondary levels. Similarly, economic fringe benefits increased, often dramatically, in terms of the proportion of boards participating and the level of their contributions.

Gains in the Level I job protection clauses also increased, from inclusion in 50 per cent of 1975–6 contracts to 100 per cent in 1984–5. Brimer comments that a notable feature of these provisions is that the criterion for determining who was surplus or redundant was brought into conformity with industrial union practice, i.e., a simply seniority measure as distinct from a professional qualification and assessment measure.

While there were no special provisions for easing or sharing the burden of redundancies in the 1975–6 agreements, by 1984–5 some 30 per cent of the agreements contained job-sharing clauses, 40 per cent included early-retirement arrangements, and 80 per cent had established deferred salary leave arrangements.

Evidence of Level II 'professional development and recognition' priorities was also ascertained. This included a 28 per cent *de-*

crease in contract provisions for professionally relevant leaves and a significant decline in higher levels of professional-qualification recognition relative to basic salaries.

So far as Level III 'professional control' issues were concerned, Brimer found counter-professional 'management rights' clauses had increased from nil in the 1975–6 agreements to an inclusion rate of 60 per cent in the elementary contracts and 20 per cent in the secondary contracts by 1984–5. Significantly, 50 per cent of the 1984–5 contracts also specified criteria by which the school administration could withhold pay increments as a disciplinary sanction, thus short-circuiting any professional peer review procedures.

Clearly the success in achieving Level I economic and job security gains within the collective bargaining process was paid for in terms of Level II, professional recognition, and Level III, professional control losses.

Brimer summarizes her findings as follows:

It appears from this analysis that Level I goals have received a great deal of attention over the past nine years, and Levels II and III much less so ... It is the achievement of Level III [professional] goals which has proven to be most problematic. These goals, in their attempt to gain some control over educational policy, threaten the traditional authority of management.

The very nature of union/management organization decreases the likelihood of teachers effectively bargaining for professional power. Union/management is a very adversarial relationship, based on rigid categories of 'management' and 'labour.' Shared decision-making would complicate this relationship by weakening these distinctions ... This idea of 'management as enemy' is very important. Unionization tends to result in an environment of conflict and confrontation. Yet shared authority requires a co-operative, consultative approach to problems if it is to be effective. It is difficult to imagine using both these labour strategies in the same work setting. Indeed, it appears that the dynamics of one ... negate the use of the other ...

Teachers turned to unionization because they did not have professional power. The evidence suggests that they will have difficulty using this new strategy to establish such professional control. (35–8)

THE LIMITS OF CONFRONTATION

At best, the distribution of social power is an unstable arrangement between various competing and co-operating interests. When-

ever an interest group perceives that its power base is inadequate
for the attainment or maintenance of its goals, it may choose to
confront those who stand directly in its path, or it may seek co-
operative support from those who may less directly influence the
broader mechanisms through which power redistribution may be
achieved. It should now be apparent that the shift to confrontational tactics reflected the degree to which teachers felt both frustrated and isolated in their quest for both material gains and
professional recognition. But as indicated, the outcome of this
confrontational tactic has been double-edged. To the extent that
local school-boards were ill-prepared to deal with such tactics,
teacher associations made rapid economic gains. But as Brimer's
and Marcotte's studies clearly demonstrate, the confrontation
tactic also served to reinforce management control mechanisms at
the expense of the teachers' professional goals. This is hardly
surprising, since jurisdiction over the system's internal distribution
of power lay within the centralized power constellation of the
provincial ministries. Further, as these same provincial ministries
were increasingly required to close the widening gap between
rising education costs and the limits of the local property tax base,
they began to impose fiscal guidelines beyond which local boards
could not negotiate. As a consequence, the material benefits that
could be achieved by teachers through collective bargaining eventually reached a point of diminishing returns at a time when the
costs of this tactic, in terms of tarnished professional image and
community prestige, were beginning to be felt.

These observations suggest that from the teacher's perspective,
the narrowly defined teacher/board confrontational tactic has
intrinsic limits. If this conclusion is correct, then further gains (or
avoidance of losses) could only be achieved either by directly con-
fronting the state, as embodied in the provincial governmental
apparatus, or in seeking co-operative alliances with other interest
groups.

At the time of this writing there is every indication that teacher
associations are carefully considering these options. But as yet
there is no clear indication of a new national direction. Again, this
is not surprising, given the evidence discussed in Chapter Three
concerning the ambivalence to be found in the value orientations of
teachers. While Canadian teachers are on average committed to
liberal 'social justice' values, they are also strongly oriented toward
conservative 'law and order' beliefs. Thus, their former willingness

to take radical action to achieve the rights extended to other workers would seem to reflect their perception of the injustice that prevailed at a time when the society at large appeared to be putting a higher value on education than school-boards put on the services of teachers.

Unfortunately, the public has not always shared this perception of injustice. In several key teacher strikes, support was not forthcoming, even from other unions. This was particularly devastating in the case of one of the longest and most bitter teacher strikes in Canadian history. In their extensive research into the Sudbury teachers' strike, Radecki and Evans (1980) noted that

because of the strike, teachers became more militant, and defined themselves more as workers than as professionals. But in a staunchly pro-union town, the striking teachers received almost no support or sympathy ... They [the teachers] confronted the SBE [Sudbury Board of Education] alone, in almost total isolation from the larger community, from parents, and from organized labour. In addition, the concern [by teachers] over students, and the deterioration of the image of teachers as dedicated professionals, were serious matters. (iii, 136)

This highlights the fundamental problem encountered by all public service employees in utilizing the industrial strike tactic. The disruption created is not felt so much by their employers as by the public in general, and their clients in particular. The damage done is not to profits (indeed, the employing agency saves money during a strike), but to the special relationship of trust between the worker and the community.

While there is very little in the way of conclusive data available on just how teachers perceive this dilemma and what they think their associations should do about it, the Carleton University (1983) survey does provide some important insights. With regard to the current state of balance between more conservative and more radical attitudes toward industrial union tactics, there is a question set that seeks opinion on legal versus extra-legal strike activity. The first question concerns attitudes toward legal limitations on strikebreaking: 'During a strike, management should be prohibited by law from hiring workers to take the place of strikers.' The second question implies an illegal union sanction against strikebreaking: 'Striking workers are generally justified in physically preventing strikebreakers from entering the place of work.'

As Table 5.1 reveals, by the 1982–3 survey date, Canadian teachers were as strongly in favour of exercising the legal strike option as hourly paid workers. However, teachers were notably less willing than hourly paid workers and much more akin to the 'Managerial and Professional' group in their unwillingness to consider the use of 'illegal' tactics, should the legislative framework not favour their interests. This evidence emphasizes the teachers' dilemma, given that these opinions were collected at a time when several provincial governments were imposing severe legal constraints on the collective bargaining rights of public employees, including teachers.

A second set of questions in the Carleton (1983) survey deals directly with the same issues upon which Brimer's survey focused. Respondents were specifically asked how they viewed their own bargaining association's agenda in terms of non-economic priorities. The question reads as follows: 'Does your union local/collective bargaining association pay a great deal of attention, some attention, or almost no attention to this issue?' Four choices of non-economic issues were provided. These were: improving health and safety conditions at work; preventing layoffs and plant [school] closings; increasing employee participation in workplace decisions; opposing ethnic or sexual discrimination in the workplace.

Table 5.2 compares the distribution of answers from 'Teachers,' 'Managerial and Professional,' and 'Hourly Paid' occupational categories. Clearly, the teachers' own subjective assessment of their bargaining association's high priority on security (2nd rank order) and lowest priority on achieving professional level participation in program and policy decisions (4th rank order) closely parallels Brimer's objective measures.

Yet there is pervasive evidence that professional recognition remains a very high priority for teachers who must now recognize that the potential for further economic gain is strictly limited in the foreseeable future. It can be logically suggested that teachers and their associations will become less narrowly economic and increasingly political in their tactics.

This politicization of teacher associations has, to a significant degree, already occurred in several jurisdictions where provincial legislation has been perceived by teachers to be particularly punitive. The tactics employed so far have been both confrontational and coalitional. On the confrontational side, teacher associations have followed the lead of other public employee unions in trying to force reversals in restrictive government legislation. There have been a number of cases where provincial teacher associations have openly backed an opposition party during an election on just such an issue (e.g., Martell 1974). On the coalitional side, there is some recent evidence of new alliances being forged between such former combatants as teacher associations and local school-boards in an effort to regain local control over public education decision-making. Just how far and in what direction this politicization of teacher organizations will go is hard to say. But, given the very real potential, it is appropriate to examine the political environment which affects public education in Canada.

6

The Political Environment

In most liberal democratic societies, public education comes under the direct jurisdiction of the state. Canada is no exception. However, jurisdiction is one thing, control another. First, the concept of the state is a holistic abstraction that encompasses a number of more fragmentary realities. In a federal system, the powers of the state are divided between local, regional, and national governments. Second, the state has both political and administrative branches. The political aspect of state power is based on an electoral constituency mandate, whereas the administrative function is extensively mediated by layers of delegated authority. In theory, policy is established at the political level and implemented at the bureaucratic level. In practice, these divisions are not always so clear-cut.

With regard to the state's divided jurisdiction, the British North America Act unambiguously ceded control over public education to the provincial level of government. While the federal government has established its 'interest' in public education through the Education Support Division of the Department of the Secretary of State, its role has necessarily been passive, in essence limited to fiscal transfers, in relation to the provinces' active jurisdiction. In summarizing this 'silent partner' relationship between the federal and provincial levels of government, Seymour Wilson (1977) notes: 'By the late 1960s a rapidly evolving pattern was set in motion. The federal government, through its involvement in massive expenditures of transfer payments, indicated its recognition of the central importance of education in Canadian society ... Placed in a comparative perspective with other western liberal democracies ... Canadians are the world's biggest spenders on education ... Furthermore, a higher percentage of the Canadian population attends school than that of any other nation' (40–4).

The evidence in support of these laudatory remarks is indeed impressive. Tables 6.1 through 6.4 reveal the extent to which Canada has committed its wealth and its youth to public education. Briefly summarized, during the period of maximum expansion, Canada increased public education's proportion of total government expenditures from 14 per cent to nearly 23 per cent (Figure 6.1 and Table 6.1). By 1969, this level of spending moved Canada into first place among all nations in terms of the proportion of GNP (8.3 per cent) that it was spending on public education (Table 6.2). Although much of this increase was because of the baby boom, which by 1970 saw nearly 40 per cent of the total population falling within the school-aged segment, to a great extent this fiscal commitment also reflected the nation's ideological commitment to education as the post-modern catalyst of economic development (Economic Council of Canada, 1964, 1965). However, as with all ideologically motivated policies, it has not been easy to abandon these commitments in light of subsequent realities. As a consequence, Canada continued to commit to public education a proportionally growing share of its national wealth (Figure 6.2), *even after the enrolments began to decline* (Figure 6.3).

A disaggregation of this overall expenditure on education reveals that although much of the increase was related to the growth in post-secondary participation rates that occurred in the 1960s, the elementary and secondary proportion remained at over 65 per cent of the total from the mid-1960s on (Figure 6.4). In terms of public jurisdictions the proportion of the federal government's *direct* contributions remained fairly stable from the 1960s into the 1980s, while municipal contributions have declined. As a consequence, the provincial proportion of all government spending on education increased between 1960 and 1980 (Figure 6.5 and Table 6.4).

But, as Katz (1974) comments, despite this overwhelming commitment to public education, 'Canada has the distinction of being the only advanced nation in the world without a federal office of education' (7). Although various attempts were made to establish such a federal bureau of education dating from 1892 (Chation 1977), federal-provincial relations were never sufficiently amicable to get the necessary agreement from the provincial governments. As a consequence, Seymour Wilson (1977) concludes his assessment of 'Federal Perspectives on Education' by noting that 'Canada has no co-ordinated educational policy and is unlikely to achieve such now or in the distant future. Therefore, provinces will continue attempting to clarify their [educational] objectives while the federal government will do likewise by pursuing a plethora of [alternative] policies having enormous implication for education throughout the land – general economic policy, regional development policy, manpower policy, social policy and foreign policy, to name only a few' (55).

When the Organization for Economic Development and Cooperation (OECD), of which Canada is a member, conducted an 'external examination' on the state of educational development in member countries, its report on Canada was even more devastating (OECD 1976). The OECD's primary criticism was that Canada has no national education policy, and that had hoc administration rather than sustained political initiative characterized provincial governmental stewardship over the world's most proportionally expensive and extensive public education system. The OECD examiners recommended the creation of improved mechanisms for interprovincial and federal-provincial accountability and co-operation.

Five years after the report was submitted, one of the outside examiners returned to evaluate the response to the OECD recommendations. His observation was that the status quo had not been significantly altered as a result of this major independent study (Hamm-Brucher 1981). The follow-up report then concluded that the continuing federal-provincial political stalemate would ensure that de facto control over public education would remain firmly entrenched within the provincial education bureaucracies.

Just how these educational bureaucracies typically function has been studied by Housego (1972):

Legislators are very little involved in determining the content of education policy decisions, which is developed rather by the 'invisible politics' of select unofficial interest groups presided over by officials of the department of education.

A peculiar quasi-official organization, then, appears to exist to allow for policy development beneath the level of the Cabinet, more specifically beneath the Minister of Education. It is made up of interest groups that are intensely self-centered; they work, however, in a form of 'coalition' that is largely initiated and maintained by the department of education ... itself one of the interest groups in the conflict.

Thus the politics of education is a politics of low visibility and informal agreement. This implies that no visible political mechanisms exist for provoking discussion and debate; that no provision exists for legitimate public dissent ... [T]here occur fewer exchanges of ideas, people, group wishes, and information between the ... system and its constituency ... The politics of education may be approaching a closed system. (15, 20, 21)

Cistone (1972) sees 'this boundary-maintaining strategy of isolating the public education system from its environment [as] a function of the ideology that schools should be politics-free ... [and because] the attitudes and sentiments of people toward education are shaped by the nature of the political order.' But these attitudes have become increasingly hostile as the public perceives educational policy, both fiscal and curricular, as being exercised within 'the privileged sanctuary of its private preserve ... [where] school boards ... chiefly perform the function of legitimating the policies of the school administration to the community' (2–3).

This is hardly the role which elected representatives of the level of educational governance that is closest to the community was intended to play. Not surprisingly, school-board trustees are sometimes resentful, if not always well appraised, of the source of their impotency. Yet, despite the evidence (e.g., Holdaway 1970) that the agendas of many elected trustees have little to do with what is going on in the schools, Bargen (1972) argues that, given 'the tremendous current pressures ... of professionalization, institutionalization and centralization' within the public school system, the direct involvement of school trustees in educational policy-making is the only means of 'preventing education from becoming imbedded in the enveloping fabric of absurdity' (75, 79).

Bergen's concern over the potential for absurdity has occasionally manifested itself in high-profile conflicts when locally elected trustees have attempted to pursue education priorities that are contrary to official policy. A rather notorious example of this occurred in 1985 when one provincial minister of education unilaterally dismissed the elected boards in two school districts, including the largest urban centre, for failing to conform to departmental policies (*Globe and Mail*, 8 May 1985, p. 9, 'Teachers support ... '; and 17 May 1985, 'Trustee's letter ... '). While the elected board argued that they were only responding to the wishes of their constituents in protecting popular programs, their replacement by a ministry-appointed caretaker trustee served to remind all concerned that local school-boards derive their authority less from their accountability to the constituency that elects them than from their delegated role as local administrators of education department policy.

Nor has the steady increase in the per capita costs of public education delivery, which has outstripped the capacity of the municipal property tax base, helped the power position of local boards. In picking up the fiscal slack (see table 6.4) provincial departments of education have felt increasingly justified in laying down universally binding guidelines on everything from building standards to library budgets. But as one study reveals, the departmental priorities tend to favour capital expenditures which mould in concrete their own organizational priorities (Bezeau 1980). Nowhere has this been more apparent than in the numerous examples of local resistance to departmental policies aimed at shutting down smaller rural or urban neighbourhood schools in favour of large, centralized mega-schools that are more 'efficient' to run administratively, but which create physical and social distance problems for students and parents.

While the accumulated evidence (as discussed earlier) shows local boards as unwilling or unable to confront either the bureaucratic power of the central ministries or the collective power of teacher associations, the most recent evidence suggests that (as in the example cited above) at least some of the larger urban board elections are being contested on education issues in response to constituency concerns over programs, teacher quality, and school proximity issues. However, it is too early to anticipate any widespread political revitalization of local school-boards.

Not all the causal factors for the apparently growing impotency of local boards can be attributed to being outflanked by the power of teacher organizations and bureaucratic authority. As Hodgson (1972) comments, 'Trustees glory in being independent; so they are often miserably independent. They value their ability to cut costs;

so they never build up a strong central office. That is, they refuse to buy the brains and the time of those people who will help to give them political clout' (69). In the absence of such clout, locally elected trustees are hardly in any position to adequately fulfil their mandate of community representation.

PRIVATE ALTERNATIVES

Since public education touches the lives of almost everyone, its conduct must be accepted as the legitimate concern of all citizens. It follows, then, that those who administer public education in the absence of clear and sustained political policy are among the most *potentially* vulnerable of public servants. It is in this light that the strong boundary-maintenance tendencies of the 'closed system' of educational administration noted above may be somewhat more sympathetically understood.

However, any presumption that all but a minority of the public take anything but a superficial interest in the school system they so generously support would be unwarranted. If, as was argued in Chapter Two, the public school system as we know it today had its birth in the 1960s, then far from being battered by public opinion, public education has been rather like a spoiled child that was given whatever it fancied by an indulgent, but not very understanding, patron. While the excessive idealism that characterized the birth of this system has now passed into a more sceptical maturity, the public's willingness to sustain, if no longer to indulge, its educational system seems reasonably secure. Indeed, to the extent that broadly representative public-opinion samples reveal a consensus, the Canadian population appears to be more willing than their elected representatives to continue paying the price of quality and accessibility of public education (Livingston 1979, 1981; Livingston & Hart 1980; Murray 1979).

This notwithstanding, there is a vocal and growing minority that is questioning the efficacy of contemporary public schooling. Although there have always been dissenters, the current criticism is not characterized, as was typical in the past, by the extravagantly polarized debates between anti-intellectual Philistines on the right and reformist intellectuals on the left. On the contrary, the contemporary public education critics are for the most part the traditionally advantaged clients of the system: professional parents, employers, post-secondary educators, even the more ambitious students.

To be sure, some of this criticism is outright scapegoating. Those who saw in the educational reforms of the 1960s the solution to all of society's most fundamental problems tend now to condemn public education's failure to deliver that which was never in its power to achieve in the first place. Nor should anyone be surprised when formerly liberal-minded, middle-class parents reverse their equality of educational opportunity ideology to join the conservative back-to-basics movement, especially with respect to early selectivity and streaming. After all, the advantages of birth take on more significance when it is realized that there is much less 'room at the top' than was once thought.

But as significant as these philosophical debates are, they fail to address the institutional problem that lies at the root of both teacher dissatisfaction and public concern: specifically, the school system's inability to address the real participation needs of frontline workers and of the concerned public. Teachers remain frustrated in their attempts to make their work environment more professionally responsible, while the public continues to be excluded from meaningful input into the important issues.

The school system's inability to accommodate non-bureaucratic participation was exemplified in the fate of the populist 'community school movement' that sprang up in the 1970s. Like those who promoted community medical clinics and legal aid services, community school advocates sought to increase the power and involvement of the client constituency, relative to either professional or bureaucratic authority. Although open to a number of interpretations – from a minimal sharing of the school's physical facilities to an almost complete merging of school and community (Nelson 1973) – the more ambitious attempts to involve the community in the school, and the school in the community, have been evaluated as not very successful (e.g., MacIver 1973). Hodgson (1972) suggests that as an attempt to 'manage disagreement' between the 'closed system' of administration and the client community's need for involvement, the concept was bound to fail precisely because it so directly threatened the high levels of boundary maintenance that lie at the core of the realpolitik of the public education system.

In any event, those disenchanted parents who have the resources are moving away from public school reform and toward support for private alternatives (Richards 1978). While the image of the private schools that survived the democratization of education is that of a closed preserve of the elite (Maxwell & Maxwell 1971; Weinzweig 1977), the emergence in the 1980s of a renewed interest in private education among the nation's middle class has given impetus to a wider range of options. Although the diversity here is considerable, the common features of the private, fee-charging school would appear to be:

- a broadening of the social and ethnic base of the clientele;
- clearly articulated educational priorities that stress fundamentals, but also include a range (depending on specific schools) of ethical and moral concerns;
- close liaison with, and involvement of, parents in school policies and activities;
- exclusion of any administrative 'authority' beyond the school and the home;
- greater accountability to clients, but also more professional freedom for a teaching staff that may be recruited and rewarded on the basis of personal qualities and performance rather than just credentials and seniority.

As Figure 6.6 reveals, while the overall school enrolments declined by 15 per cent in the decade following their 1970 peak, private school enrolments increased by nearly 60 per cent. Although the absolute numbers of students attending private schools remains relatively small (220,000 by 1981), the rapid increase may well predict a much more prominent role for private education in the future.

This trend has been reinforced within several provincial jurisdictions which are now providing public subsidy for private education (Brown 1980). The amounts involved are not insignificant. In British Columbia, for example, public support of private education grew from 2.6 per cent to 28 per cent of the private education budget between 1972 and 1982. This trend has raised strong protests from within the public education establishment and from teacher associations who feel threatened that any significant 'privatization' of educational delivery would diminish their own power base.

Perhaps even more indicative of the willingness of governments to support alternatives to their own education systems has been

Ontario's controversial decision to put its religiously based 'separate' school system on fiscal parity with the public system. Although initially interpreted as a gesture by the government of the day to the province's Catholic community, the proviso that public financial support would only be forthcoming if the separate school system opened its doors to any who wanted to come suggests a broader political motivation. In essence, what Ontario has created is two publicly supported and publicly accessible school systems, only one of which is controlled by the public education bureaucracy. The resulting redistribution of school property and teaching staff from the public to the separate system only served to accelerate the contraction of the former and the expansion of the latter. Not surprisingly, this produced much tension and much complaint from those negatively affected. However, for the most part the appeal for public support by advocates of the public system fell on deaf ears.

It is not possible at this writing to predict the full consequences of the growing interest in private alternatives to state-administered education. It is doubtful that it will ever come close to the extreme 'new right' advocacy, which argues for the total closure of the public system with the state's obligation limited to the issuing of education 'vouchers' to all citizens who may then 'cash them in' as part or full payment in a free market-place of private schools (Jencks 1970; LaNoue 1971). However, the trend toward more direct public subsidy of private education may be motivated as much by growing public concern with public school accountability as by a carry-over of elitist thinking. However, the concerns of those who maintain faith in public education as a prime instrument of social equity are justified by the evidence that private options, publicly funded or not, tend to reinforce existing social inequalities. From the perspective of public school teachers these same privatization trends may well appear to be less a political response to public disenchantment over accountability issues than part of a wider 'contracting out' trend through which public-sector workers are made to carry a disproportionate share of the fiscal-constraint burden.

Whatever the underlying motives and eventual outcome of these alternative education trends, their very emergence underscores, without promising to resolve, the growing occupational problems of schoolteachers, the policy problems of school administration, and the educational accountability problems of the public.

7

Education, Pedagogy, and the Public Interest

Public schooling, as we understand it today, had its origins in the industrial revolution. The notion that everyone has both a right and an obligation to obtain a basic education has two rather contradictory bases. On the one hand, modern industrial society requires that all citizens hold *in common* certain basic cognitive skills and social attitudes. On the other hand, industrial society also demands an *uncommon* diversity of specialized knowledge and occupational functions. The contradictions inherent in this dualism are further reinforced by the paradoxes of liberal-democratic ideology which is committed at one and the same time to the amelioration of socially derived inequality and the facilitation of differential economic rewards.

The principal philosophical construct through which these contradictions are rationalized is the concept of a 'meritocracy.' here it is argued that everyone should have 'equal opportunity' to compete for the unequal rewards that are so ubiquitously promoted within societies with liberal economies (Bell 1977). However, the notion that compulsory school attendance could by itself achieve significant redistribution of wealth and privilege is either naive or a deception. Nevertheless, this ideology lies at the root of the multi-branched public education debate.

To understand these intrinsic contradictions is also to recognize the irreducible residue of conflict that lies behind the continuing search for consensus on public education that characterizes all western industrial societies (Coombs 1985). For public education in industrial societies is not simply a means for making formal knowledge publicly accessible; it is also an agent of political socialization, social valorization, cultural reproduction, and labour-force allocation, and as the latter became increasingly problematic, a warehouse for the containment of youthful unemployables.

The nation's schools are thus facilitators and gatekeepers; providers and rationers; emancipators and custodians; critics and propagandists. That such a system produces both 'winners and losers' (Anisef et al 1982), and labels them accordingly, should surprise no-one who understands its fundamental dialectics. But neither should anyone be surprised that because of this there will always be a debate over public education policy in general, and instructional content and methods in particular. Given these intrinsic tensions, it should be self-evident that neither the public school system as an institution nor teachers as an occupational group could expect to develop and maintain any non-publicly-accountable basis of autonomous authority. But this is not to suggest that the school and its teachers should not have some independent basis of authority through which their fragile integrity can be maintained, especially during periods of social upheaval.

It is, of course, during those critical points in history, when the established economic model, social traditions, and cultural values seem no longer to produce their intended results, that the basis of authority of the school, and those who teach within the school, becomes most vulnerable to attack from competing interests. As John Macdonald (1970) put it in his thoughtful study *The Discernible Teacher*, 'when society has just renewed itself, the school is an alchemic laboratory; when the model of social action has worked itself out, the school is closer to a prison, with the guardian teachers more prisoner than their charges.'

The abiding consensus, then, is that public schooling is widely accepted as both desirable and necessary. The conflict that persistently threatens the system's fragile checks and balances, particularly during times of wider socio-economic trauma, arises out of the lack of agreement on how to expedite that consensus. Although such ideologically based conflict can have no ultimate resolution, operational consensus is attainable on the basis of a broad public trust in the judgment, competence, and integrity of those responsible for delivering the service.

If, however, this public trust should substantially fail, not only is the basis of the authority of teachers put in jeopardy, but the whole public education enterprise becomes diminished, as the most talented teachers, competent administrators, concerned parents, and involved students abandon the public education system for more viable alternatives.

PEDAGOGY: THE SEARCH FOR AUTHORITY

The concept of authority is rooted in the notion that those who wield power exercise their prerogatives with the consent of the subject population. Beginning with Max Weber's (1947) seminal work, there has been wide interest in identifying the means by which such consent may be achieved. Briefly summarized, these consensual mechanisms are:

TRADITIONAL – authority reflects the passive acceptance of *dynastic* power arrangements.
CHARISMATIC – authority derives from the *personal* magnetism of born leaders.
LEGAL-RATIONAL – authority proceeds from the formal *rule* structure attached to bureaucratic office.
POLITICAL – authority arises out of a *constituency-based* mandate.
PROFESSIONAL – authority is claimed as a consequence of a special public *trust* in an area of serviceable *knowledge* application.

As modern industrial social organization developed, a progressive reduction in the 'traditional' and the 'charismatic' bases of authority has been paralleled by a growth in constituency-based 'political' and bureaucratically based 'rational-legal' forms. The 'professional' form also expanded for a time (as discussed in Chapter One), particularly in those human service areas that did not easily submit to political and/or bureaucratic control mechanisms. But as large-scale organization eventually overtook the human service field and as 'welfare state' policies enjoyed increasing popularity in the context of growing public concern over professional accountability, the professional basis of authority legitimation declined in favour of power-sharing arrangements with various private 'sponsors' or public 'mediators' (Johnson 1972; Schon 1983).

The effect of these wider changes on the authority of teachers has been to remove their once-dominant basis of authority without providing access to alternative forms. Students, parents, and even teachers themselves are no longer prepared to play by the closed-rank rules of *in loco parentis* – rules which once assured teachers a 'traditional' basis of authority by virtue of their accepted coequality with parents in the matter of raising children 'strictly' on the assumption of adult infallibility.

Further, a whole new structure of legal rights for children now challenges the once military-like omnipotence of the school's rational-legal basis of authority (Bargen 1961; Berkeley et al. 1978; Gaffield & West 1978). For example, Canada's new human rights legislation has brought into question whether school personnel have the authority to invoke any but the mildest sanctions without legally transgressing the newly acquired right of children to due process.

Further, there cannot be much doubt, given the evidence discussed in this study, that Canadian teachers have never had any real opportunity to establish what Johnson (1972) calls a 'producer-controlled, collegiate' basis of professional autonomy and self-regulation. While the client-delegated, 'patronage' model of professionalism is undoubtedly the basis of the private school teacher's parent-delegated authority (Weinzweig 1977), the same degree of professional autonomy and parental involvement or trust cannot be expected within a public school system that so completely isolates teachers and parents from each other and then excludes both from administrative decision-making.

This isolation of teachers from their client constituency has been further deepened by the predominant negotiation strategy of teacher associations. Recognizing the drift toward centralized bureaucratic control, these associations have followed the time-honoured strategy of seeking to negotiate at the same level of organized power as those who make the real decisions. But this real decision-making power constellation is none other than the same remote state apparatus that has largely succeeded in eliminating public involvement in favour of the closed system of consensus management.

If, as Housego (1972) has argued, the emergence of this closed system is due to the absence of effective community-based political mediation, then its continuation at a time when costs are escalating, demand declining, and concerns over quality and purpose are growing can only fuel public concern for greater accountability. But the question must be asked: accountability for what and to whom? Since public education now performs so many functions, some of which are at odds, the 'for what' question would seem to be a matter of pressing policy concern. The question of accountability 'to whom' once again brings the issue of the basis of authority into the forefront. Traditional authority is accountable to past practice; bureaucratic authority is accountable to the formal rule structure; professional authority is accountable to collegial peers at one level and client interests at another; political authority is accountable to its constituency. Given the organization of public education as we have come to understand it, where does the teacher's responsibility lie and in what way does this responsibility differ from that of the school, the local board, and the ministry's levels of administration? Without clear answers to these questions, neither teachers nor administrators are likely to willingly lay themselves open to public scrutiny.

Thus, if parents and other interested public groups cannot effectively communicate with teachers; if locally elected trustees are reduced to little more than puppets of remote bureaucratic decision-makers; if senior governments are politically hamstrung by jurisdictional divisions and by the very size, complexity, and longevity of their own public administrative apparatus; and if this administrative apparatus must, in the absence of politically informed policy directives, necessarily develop its own 'competency' around keeping the potentially explosive school and public issues separated, then no one should be surprised at the emerging crisis of authority within and beyond the classroom.

PUBLIC INTEREST: THE SEARCH FOR INTERVENTION

Viewed selectively, much of the data on teacher characteristics presented in this analysis might be construed as evidence that teachers have become overpaid for, and under-committed to, their work. But interpreted holistically, the analysis presented here strongly suggests that teachers have not yet become as cynical as other categories of knowledge workers who have been subjected to the highly bureaucratized work environments of contemporary industrial organization. For example, the data on both 'motivational' versus 'operational' and the 'is' versus 'ought' attitudes reveal a picture of, at least initially, highly motivated teachers experiencing unmanageable role conflict, performance criteria of questionable relevance, and significant levels of status inconsistency. These structurally induced problems have inevitably produced personal dissatisfaction, not all the complex sources of which are likely to be understood by those affected. The result has been teacher frustration, which has led in good times to high levels of defection and in bad times to high levels of conflict.

Most certainly, if teachers are subjected to the same alienating forces experienced by other industrial workers, it must also be expected that they too will be forced, often reluctantly, to abandon socially responsible goals in order to pursue economic goals, which the collective bargaining process so singularly promotes. But if the recently better-educated and more rigorously selected teachers remain frustrated over their exclusion from the decision processes that determine their occupational satisfaction, so too has a more enlightened public remained frustrated over their exclusion from participation in public education policy-making. This dual frustration, which appears to stem from the same source, has all too commonly resulted in conflicts which pit teacher 'demands' against public 'indignation.' Since both teachers and the public have been denied access to the level of decision-making that could in any significant way resolve their mutual frustration, this teacher/community conflict has not led to innovative resolution.

As a consequence of their vulnerability to uninformed public attacks, teachers have tended to reinforce the closed system of administration. For it is this system that assures them of such basic protections as tenure and seniority rights. Reactive public interest groups, such as British Columbia's 'Genuine Education Movement' (GEM), have tended to respond with demands for more direct intervention, not only in educational policy but hiring and firing of teachers. The great pity is that many of those with political responsibility have simply exploited public frustration by imposing blanket fiscal restraint policies, leaving the reallocative policies to the 'closed system of administration.' Needless to say, such fiscal cut-backs that are not accompanied by a public policy

review process through which long-range priorities are established
are bound to produce more heat than light among those who must
live with the resulting chaos.

If the public's concern over its exclusion from educational content and delivery is only able to find its voice in glib editorial comment, and its political expression only in support for reactive fiscal
cut-backs, it is hard to imagine any very satisfactory outcome.
Certainly, if the evidence and analysis presented here carry any
conviction, it is that the public's interest in educating the young
would be better served by making teachers more professionally
accountable as dedicated and knowledgeable *educators*. However,
the current trend is to hold them increasingly accountable for
managing, or containing, a growing list of non-educative social
control functions and social service problems that other institutions seem no longer able to address. But if teachers are expected
to perform as social workers, employment agents, drug and alcohol
abuse counsellors, public health clinicians, day-care supervisors to
latch-key kids, and custodians of unemployable young adults – all
the while ensuring there are no messy public relations problems –
then clearly the system should train them, and the public should
judge them, accordingly. But surely that is not what the public, if it
were to consider the matter seriously, would want or realistically
expect of its schoolteachers.

If such a purely educative basis for teacher accountability were
established, and if appropriate teacher and public involvement
were assured, a serious restructuring of the whole teaching career
system would surely be a consequence. Such a reshaping might
include:

– Finding ways of raising the status of teaching to something
  more than the bottom rung of a career ladder, where 'success'
  leads out of the classroom.
– Ensuring a better balance between the socially stabilizing humanistic foundations of any worthwhile pedagogy and the chao-
  tically shifting instrumental skill imperatives of an ever more
  turbulent economy.
– Reducing the severe role conflicts that undercut the educative
  authority of teachers by strictly limiting any requirement that
  they act as agents for outside systems of authority.

- Providing meaningful opportunities to exercise publicly observable educative judgment at a more fundamental and intellectually stimulating level than the delivering of pre-digested curricula in the classroom.

While the analysis presented here offers ample justification for consideration of all the above changes, it is the last which should command the most attention. For as Henchey (1977) has argued, teachers will inevitably be perceived as 'undervalued and overpaid if all they have to do is make the meals using someone else's recipe book ... [this implies] the transformation of professional responsibility from custodial care, the enforcement of compulsory school attendance, and the sorting and certifying of the youth to a more service-oriented profession which attempts to enlighten rather than direct the choices which its clients must make and which provides the resources to help them realize their choices' (155).

But having noted this, it is also important to remind teachers that when it comes to the really fundamental questions, the public considers education too important a business to be left entirely to educators. It would therefore be unwise for teachers to aspire to a full 'collegiate' level of professional control. But the evidence also suggests that teachers do not in fact seek such a level of autonomy. However, in being forced to concede virtually all curricular and organizational policy control to the 'closed system' of administration, and to rely so exclusively upon the client-insensitive collective bargaining process to negotiate their occupational interests, teachers have severely limited the options through which their own professional needs and the legitimate interests of their host community could be more directly mediated.

To be sure, such a meeting of professional and public interests would not in and of itself ensure consensus on matters of policy. But should such a community-based forum develop, the differences are much more likely to cut across than down the teacher-public division. Thus, the 'irreducible conflict' that is inherent in the public education enterprise would be rendered more amenable to creative compromise. Indeed, what distinguishes *community-based* political mediation from centralized bureaucratic administration is the former's potential for rendering the real sources of conflict publicly accessible.

These, then, would appear to be the public policy implications of this attempt to develop a comprehensive analysis of the particular properties of public school teaching as this occupation has struggled to keep pace with complex forces of change. Although the evidence available never tells the whole story, and any analytic interpretation is quite properly open to critical questioning, there can be little doubt that some serious problems exist within the career system of public school teachers. It seems equally apparent that unless these problems are effectively dealt with in the near future, public education in Canada is likely to suffer an escalating crisis of confidence.

Tables

TABLE 2.1
Increase in teaching-force in comparison with other demographic and institutional
variables, Canada, 1955–80

	1955 base	1960	1965	1970	1975	1980
Elem. & sec. teachers						
(N = x1000)	123.8	164.0	211.8	272.3	281.0	276.3
% change since base year		32	71	120	127	123
% change since previous interval		32	29	29	3	−2
Elem. & sec. enrolments						
(N = x1000)	3,291.4	4,204.4	5,201.3	5,836.1	5,594.7	5,106.3
% change since base year		28	58	77	70	55
% change since previous interval		28	24	12	−4	−10
Total population						
(N = x1000)*	16,081	18,238	20,015	21,568	22,993	24,574
% change since base year		13	24	34	42	53
% change since previous interval		13	10	8	7	7
Retention rate (7%)						
14–17 year olds	53.5	66.2	79.6	87.9	85.0	85.0
Student/teacher ratio	26.6	25.6	24.6	21.4	19.9	18.5

SOURCE: SC 81-210, 81-220, 81-229, 81-568, 81-569, 11-402
* For census years 1956, 1961, 1966, 1971, 1976, and 1981

TABLE 3.1
Percentage of teachers who are female, Canada
(excluding Quebec), 1955–83

Year	Elementary	Secondary	All
1955	80	36	70
1960	79	33	72
1965	77	34	63
1970	75	35	61
1975	69	32	55
1980	66	30	53
1983	66	31	54

SOURCE: SC 81-202

TABLE 3.2
Percentage of all teachers who are male compared
with percentage of all students enrolled at the
secondary level, Canada, 1955–80

Year	Male teachers	Students in secondary school
1955	27	15
1960	29	19
1965	34	23
1970	38	30
1975	42	34
1980	44	35

Correlation coefficient = .99
Coefficient of determination = .98

SOURCE: SC 81-202, 81-229, 81-568

TABLE 3.3
Ethnic distribution of Canadian schoolteachers
compared with population as a whole

Ethnic group	Teachers (%)	Population (%)
United Kingdom	55.8	44.6
French	18.7	28.7
U.K. & French	74.5	73.3
All others	25.6	26.7

SOURCE: Special run, Carleton University (1983),
Canadian Class Structure survey, SC 11-420

TABLE 3.4
Socio-economic status origins of teacher-education students compared with all other university students, Canada, 1969, 1975, and 1983

Father's status level:		Upper/Upper Middle			Middle			Lower middle			Lower		
Year of student survey:		1969	1975	1983	1969	1975	1983	1969	1975	1983	1969	1975	1983
Male only	Teacher ed (E) %	6.0	12.3	24.5	12.0	14.3	15.9	10.3	13.8	20.6	71.8	59.7	38.9
	All others (O) %	18.4	20.8	29.0	17.2	18.7	18.0	15.0	15.2	20.5	49.4	45.3	32.5
	E/O	0.3	0.6	0.8	0.7	0.8	0.9	0.7	0.9	1.0	1.5	1.3	1.2
Female only	Teacher ed (E) %	12.9	15.5	24.2	20.6	17.3	19.0	13.9	12.3	22.6	52.5	54.8	34.3
	All others (O) %	23.0	23.5	30.4	20.4	19.9	20.1	12.7	15.3	17.5	43.7	41.3	32.0
	E/O	0.6	0.7	0.8	1.0	0.9	0.9	1.1	0.8	1.3	1.2	1.3	1.1
Male & female	Teacher ed (E) %	10.0	14.3	24.3	17.0	16.0	17.9	12.3	13.0	21.8	60.4	56.7	35.8
	All others (O) %	19.8	21.8	29.5	18.2	19.3	18.8	14.3	15.2	19.4	47.6	43.7	32.3
	E/O	0.5	0.7	0.8	0.9	0.8	1.0	0.9	0.9	1.1	1.3	1.3	1.1

SOURCE: Post-secondary student population surveys, 1968/9, 1974/5, 1982/3

TABLE 3.5
Teaching-force, mean-age, and median-years of experience,
Canada (excluding Quebec), 1955–83

Year	Mean age	Median experience	Annualarized rate of enrolment change since previous interval (%)
1955	n.a.	7.8	base
1960	n.a.	8.0	5.6
1965	n.a.	6.6	4.8
1970	35*	7.3	2.4
1975	35	8.0	−0.8
1980	37	10.0	−5.0
1983	39	12.0	−1.0

SOURCE: SC 81-202, 81-220
* 1972 data substituted for missing 1970 data.

TABLE 3.6
Percentage of all teachers in early, middle, and
late career divisions, Canada (excluding Quebec),
1972–83

Year	Under 34	35–49	Over 50
1972	61	26	13
1974	59	28	13
1975	57	31	12
1976	55	33	12
1977	53	34	13
1978	51	35	14
1979	48	39	13
1981	42	45	13
1983	34	52	14

SOURCE: SC 81-569, 81-202

TABLE 3.7
Percentage of teachers with a university degree,
Canada (excluding Quebec), 1960–83

Year	Elementary	Secondary	Total
1960	11	67	26
1965	13	73	33
1970	32	76	48
1975	49	83	61
1980	69	89	76
1983	79	93	84

SOURCE: SC 81-202, 81-569

TABLE 3.8
Percentage of bachelors graduates from different fields of
study who became teachers two years after graduation,
Canada, 1969 and 1976 graduating classes

Field of study	Graduating year	% who became teachers
Education	1969	92.3
	1976	82.5
Business/Commerce	1969	5.0
	1976	8.0
Fine Arts	1969	70.4
	1976	46.5
Humanities	1969	60.5
	1976	52.1
Social Sciences	1969	37.4
	1976	33.6
Biological Science/ Agriculture	1969	45.9
	1976	26.0
Engineering/ Applied Science	1969	6.4
	1976	5.0
Health	1969	14.1
	1976	4.3
Maths/ Physical Science	1969	42.1
	1976	26.9
General	1969	52.7
	1976	39.3
Total % of all graduates who became teachers	1969	50.4
	1976	41.2
Total % of non- education majors who became teachers	1969	39.4
	1976	29.7

SOURCE: Picot, 1983: Table 8

TABLE 3.9
University graduates who entered teaching as first full-time job, teachers compared
with other occupational fields, by graduating group and highest degree, Canada,
1950–73

Graduating group		School- teaching %	University & college %	Health & welfare %	Admini- stration %	Busi- ness %	Manufac- turing %	Other %
1950–4	Bach.	18.2	2.7	16.5	9.2	11.4	18.3	23.7
	Mast.	16.6	10.9	18.5	19.9	3.9	8.1	22.5
	PhD	6.7	36.5	9.0	24.1	5.7	9.3	9.7
1955–9	Bach.	20.4	2.8	16.8	9.6	11.4	13.8	25.2
	Mast.	22.5	10.4	18.5	13.1	6.5	9.9	18.6
	PhD	7.5	40.3	8.2	20.0	5.1	9.6	9.3
1960–4	Bach.	32.8	3.7	14.2	7.9	9.7	11.2	19.9
	Mast.	24.6	11.9	17.5	11.9	7.7	10.3	17.1
	PhD	7.9	42.9	8.4	16.3	5.0	8.6	11.4
1965–9	Bach.	39.9	4.6	10.1	8.1	8.1	10.0	19.3
	Mast.	30.0	14.8	12.8	12.2	6.0	12.7	11.5
	PhD	9.3	46.9	6.0	14.7	6.1	7.3	9.7
1970–3	Bach.	37.0	5.0	8.9	8.8	8.2	6.4	25.7
	Mast.	32.2	17.2	9.7	11.0	5.3	12.7	12.9
	PhD	12.4	43.5	6.3	12.6	5.5	7.5	12.3

SOURCE: Special run, Highly Qualified Manpower Survey, 1973

TABLE 3.10
Liberal vs. conservative value orientations, teachers compared with other occupational groups, Canada, 1983

	Teachers		Managerial & professional		Hourly employees		Mean % Lib.	Mean % Cons.
	% Lib.	% Cons.	% Lib.	% Cons.	% Lib.	% Cons.		
1 Corporations benefit owners at expense of workers	20.2	8.2	30.5	16.9	25.9	10.9	25.5	12.8
2 Too much corporate power	36.4	4.0	37.3	7.4	48.0	4.3	40.6	5.2
3 Society could run without profits.	12.3	32.6	8.4	40.1	16.8	30.2	12.5	34.3
4 Hierarchial division of labour is necessary.	17.8	24.6	8.2	34.1	7.0	35.2	11.0	31.3
5 Management not required to run operation	20.1	23.8	8.7	40.8	16.8	30.2	15.2	31.6
6 Poverty is due to some not being intelligent enough to compete.	36.2	4.6	34.2	8.4	30.9	10.0	33.8	7.7
7 Poverty is due to lack of education and jobs.	30.6	8.6	34.9	7.1	33.5	9.6	33.0	8.4
8 Poverty is due to laziness.	29.6	6.6	18.6	15.7	22.3	24.8	23.5	15.7
9 Poverty is due to profit motive.	7.9	24.1	9.7	33.1	18.1	18.8	11.9	25.3
10 Poverty is due to necessity for social hierarchy.	23.5	8.6	25.4	12.2	16.5	19.4	21.8	13.4
11 Crime is best reduced by increasing punishment	7.6	33.9	9.1	41.7	5.0	61.7	7.2	45.8
12 Crime is best reduced through more education and jobs.	45.8	3.6	45.4	5.6	49.9	3.9	47.0	4.4
13 Crime is best reduced by increasing child discipline.	3.8	38.1	11.5	28.4	12.7	34.9	9.3	33.8

	Teachers		Managerial & professional		Hourly employees		Mean % Lib.	Mean % Cons.
	% Lib.	% Cons.	% Lib.	% Cons.	% Lib.	% Cons.		
14 Many receive less income than they deserve.	22.8	5.6	17.1	11.4	26.3	7.2	22.3	8.1
15 Should increase UIC	12.7	25.4	7.5	27.1	11.5	25.2	10.6	25.9
16 If necessary taxes should be raised to benefit pensioners.	46.5	1.8	32.3	8.4	29.8	11.1	36.2	7.1
17 Welfare wasted on those who won't work	18.7	3.2	20.1	13.4	11.8	27.0	16.9	14.5
18 Government should guarantee jobs.	40.6	4.6	40.5	8.5	58.7	4.0	46.6	5.7
19 If necessary taxes should be increased to pay for welfare programs.	30.1	2.6	24.1	10.8	29.8	11.5	28.0	8.3
Column mean	24.4	13.9	22.3	19.5	24.8	20.0	23.8	17.8

SOURCE: Special run, Carleton University (1983), Canadian Class Structure survey

TABLE 4.1
Percentage of those who began careers as teachers
who are now employed in other work (controlled
for sex, age group, and teaching level)

Age group	Primary		Secondary	
	M	F	M	F
Over 40	21	30	39	32
30–39	45	37	64	37
Under 30	76	64	73	58

SOURCE: Highly Qualified Manpower Survey,
1973

TABLE 4.2
Occupational fields entered by those who leave teaching (controlled for sex, age
group, and teaching level)

Age group & level		Managerial & professional		Sales & clerical		Skilled & unskilled	
		M %	F %	M %	F %	M %	F %
Over 40	P*	92	76	6	20	2	4
	S*	92	69	5	26	3	4
30–39	P	94	67	5	23	2	10
	S	90	77	6	15	4	8
Under 30	P	76	49	7	36	17	14
	S	67	62	19	19	14	19

SOURCE: Highly Qualified Manpower Survey, 1973
* P = primary, S = secondary

TABLE 4.3
Percentage of teachers who began full-time
employment in some other field (controlled
for sex, age group, and teaching level)

Age group	Primary		Secondary	
	M	F	M	F
Over 40	30	26	68	36
30–39	13	17	20	20
Under 30	16	10	13	14

SOURCE: Highly Qualified Manpower Survey,
1973

TABLE 4.4
Occupational origins of those who enter teaching late (controlled for sex, age group,
and teaching level)

Age group & level		Managerial & professional		Sales & clerical		Skilled & unskilled	
		M %	F %	M %	F %	M %	F %
Over 40	P*	60	50	26	33	15	22
	S*	58	60	21	27	20	14
30–39	P	47	27	27	16	26	50
	S	53	61	28	20	19	18
Under 30	P	19	41	27	51	54	8
	S	43	59	17	27	40	14

SOURCE: Highly Qualified Manpower Survey, 1973
* P = primary, S = secondary

TABLE 4.5
Distribution of teacher-education graduates by occupations entered (cohorted by
year of graduation)

Graduation cohort	Sex	Teaching %	Managerial & professional %	Clerical & sales %	Skilled & unskilled %	Other %
Pre-1945	M	48.9	38.9	5.3	7.0	–
	F	80.1	6.6	8.5	1.5	3.2
1945–9	M	49.7	30.3	7.5	12.5	–
	F	75.9	15.0	8.0	1.1	–
1950–4	M	60.9	28.4	4.9	5.8	–
	F	83.3	11.9	0.7	4.1	–
1955–9	M	61.0	25.7	8.0	5.3	–
	F	78.4	13.3	5.0	2.0	1.2
1960–4	M	69.6	22.0	2.3	6.0	–
	F	77.4	11.5	5.3	4.6	1.2
1965–9	M	74.7	18.0	3.2	3.9	0.2
	F	79.5	10.6	3.4	4.2	2.3
1970–3	M	70.5	18.9	4.4	4.7	1.4
	F	70.5	18.0	6.5	2.7	2.3

SOURCE: Special run, Highly Qualified Manpower Survey, 1973

TABLE 4.6
Annual median salary of teachers compared with annual industrial composite wage
– $ values, current and real (1971) – Canada (excluding Quebec), 1955–80

Year	Median teacher salary (current $)	Median teacher salary (T) (1971 $)	Individual composite annual wage (current $)	Individual composite wage (I) (1971 $)	Ratio T/I
1955	2,840	4,207	3,175	4,704	0.89
1956	3,162	4,616	3,351	4,892	0.94
1957	3,470	4,901	3,532	4,989	0.98
1958	3,757	5,175	3,662	5,044	1.03
1959	4,055	5,525	3,820	5,204	1.06
1960	4,247	5,716	3,943	5,307	1.08
1961	4,414	5,885	4,068	5,424	1.09
1962	4,522	5,958	4,188	5,518	1.08
1963	4,722	6,125	4,330	5,616	1.09
1964	4,954	6,303	4,499	5,724	1.10
1965	5,215	6,478	4,733	5,880	1.10
1966	5,567	6,667	5,008	5,998	1.11
1967	6,524	7,542	5,344	6,178	1.22
1968	6,497	7,219	5,714	6,349	1.14
1969	7,124	7,571	6,117	6,501	1.16
1970	7,688	7,909	6,595	6,785	1.17
1971	8,525	8,525	7,157	7,157	1.19
1972	9,600	9,160	7,759	7,404	1.24
1973	10,500	9,317	8,344	7,404	1.26
1974	11,900	9,520	9,261	7,409	1.28
1975	14,004	10,111	10,578	7,638	1.32
1976	16,615	11,158	11,858	7,964	1.40
1977	18,408	11,448	12,997	8,083	1.42
1978	20,023	11,429	13,799	7,876	1.45
1979	22,200	11,611	14,989	7,839	1.48
1980	24,877	11,812	16,504	7,837	1.51
1981	28,845	12,176	18,475	7,799	1.56
1982	32,128	12,239	19,994	7,617	1.61
1983	32,126	11,569	20,210	7,278	1.59

SOURCE: SC 72-002, 81-202, 81-569, 11-003

TABLE 4.7
Salary range and years to maximum for teachers with basic certificates, by province, 1983 agreements

Province	Negotiation jurisdiction	Minimum $	Maximum $	Years to maximum
British Columbia	Vancouver	22,654	34,255	10
Alberta	Calgary	22,745	38,420	11
Saskatchewan	Province	21,674	36,354	10
Manitoba	Winnipeg	23,199	36,020	9
Ontario	Frontenac	21,405	38,310	11
Quebec	Province	20,845	31,384	14
New Brunswick	Province	20,030	30,974	10
Nova Scotia	Province	21,287	33,997	10
Prince Edward Island	Province	17,427	27,005	10
Newfoundland	Province	22,823	30,383	9
Northwest Territories	Territory	30,487	44,271	10
Yukon	Territory	30,444	44,783	10

SOURCE: Canadian Teachers' Federation (1983)
*1982 agreement

TABLE 4.8
Average annual salary of classroom teachers compared with school administrators, Canada, 1982

	Highest maximum $	Average salary $	Average salary controlled for scale difference $
Teacher	45,598		
Elementary		32,312	35,220
Secondary		36,199	41,267
School administrator	55,085		
Elementary		44,378	
Secondary		44,890	

SOURCE: SC 202 (1983/4); Marcotte (1984)

TABLE 4.9
Individual income distribution, teachers compared with other
occupational groups, Canada, 1981

$ x1000	Teachers %	Managerial & professional %	Hourly paid %
<10	7.2	16.9	29.0
10–15	10.6	9.4	21.0*
15–20	13.6	12.8	17.0
20–25	15.8	15.9*	13.9
25–35	39.2*	18.9	12.0
35–50	12.5	15.9	4.4
50–75	1.1	7.8	1.3
75–100	–	0.9	0.7
>100	–	0.9	0.5

SOURCE: Special run, Carleton University Canadian Class
Structure survey
* Interval within which the median income occurs

TABLE 4.10
Working spouses, teachers compared with other occupational
groups, Canada, 1981

	Teachers %	Managerial & professional %	Hourly paid %
1 Now living with spouse	70.1	61.9	58.3
2 Spouse now working	74.6	63.7	58.3
3 Spouse now seeking work	13.0	20.2	22.6
(2 + 3)	87.6	83.9	80.9

SOURCE: Special run, Carleton University Canadian Class
Structure survey

TABLE 4.11
Family income distribution, teachers compared with other
occupational groups, Canada, 1981

$ x1000	Teachers %	Managerial & professional %	Hourly paid %
<25	20.4	28.9	51.4*
25–35	23.8	22.3*	21.9
35–50	25.5*	24.4	17.3
50–75	25.0	17.4	5.1
75–100	5.3	4.7	2.0
>100	–	1.8	1.3

SOURCE: Special run, Carleton University Canadian Class
Structure survey
* Interval within which the median income occurs

TABLE 4.12
Total hours worked and secondary sources of earned income, teachers compared
with other occupational groups, Canada, 1983

	Teachers	Managerial & professional	Hourly paid
Average no. hours/week devoted to primary employment*	47.8	47.4	46.8
Those pursuing extra outside earnings (%)	7.3	8.5	9.5
Those whose outside earnings are from self-employment (%)	6.4	38.4	39.8
Average no. extra hours/week spent on outside work	19	14	18

SOURCE: Special run, Carleton University Canadian Class Structure survey
* All full-time employees in each category, including overtime for hourly employees

TABLE 4.13
Perceptions of actual and preferred exercise of high-level influence by individual and
group categories, teachers compared with other occupational groups, Canada, 1983

	Teachers		Managerial & professional		Hourly paid	
	Actual %	Preferred %	Actual %	Preferred %	Actual %	Preferred %
Managers	77.5	58.4	80.4	73.6	76.6	71.0
Employee group	27.5	54.0	24.8	39.9	14.9	28.9
Union	20.8	36.1	18.7	18.2	15.2	18.6
Individual	15.2	31.6	32.9	42.0	17.9	25.1

SOURCE: Special run, Carleton University Canadian Class Structure survey

TABLE 4.14
Work autonomy responses of teachers compared with other occupational groups,
Canada, 1983

	Per cent who answered 'yes'		
Area of work autonomy	Teachers	Managerial & professional	Hourly paid
Job requires creative input	84.8	74.6	33.3
It is possible to make some creative inputs	97.0	88.3	57.8
Can decide work schedule	10.5	45.5	20.1
Can take time off without having to account to anyone	19.8	41.5	23.8
Can significantly control pace of work	45.8	56.3	40.8
Can introduce new tasks	38.7	67.9	39.7
Can decide how to do job	88.4	86.8	66.6
No direct supervision of work	18.4	26.7	18.4
Not required to report to supervisor	40.6	52.6	55.8
Mean	49.4	60.0	39.6
(SD)	(32.7)	(21.0)	(17.5)

SOURCE: Special run, Carleton University Canadian Class Structure survey

TABLE 5.1
Attitudes on legal and extra-legal strike tactics, teachers compared with other
occupational groups, Canada, 1983

	Teachers		Managerial & professional		Hourly paid	
	*SA %	SD %	SA %	SD %	SA %	SD %
Legal	44	13	30	24	44	21
Extra-legal	6	50	5	60	10	46

SOURCE: Special run, Carleton University Canadian Class Structure survey
* SA = strongly agree; SD = strongly disagree

TABLE 5.2
Membership's evaluation of union's non-economic priorities, teachers compared with
other occupational groups (per cent and rank order distributions), Canada, 1983

	Teachers		Managerial & professional		Hourly paid	
	%	RO	%	RO	%	RO
Health & safety	36.2	(3)	40.9	(2)	59.8	(1)
Stop layoffs	54.4	(2)	53.7	(1)	43.6	(2)
Discrimination	54.7	(1)	38.7	(3)	37.1	(3)
Participation	29.4	(4)	32.5	(4)	24.2	(4)

Rank order correlations: T vs. M&P   =   .20
                          T vs. HP   = −.94
                          M&P vs. HP =   .80

SOURCE: Special run, Carleton University Canadian Class Structure survey

TABLE 6.1

Distribution of total government expenditures on
major services, Canada, 1961, 1966, 1971

	1961 %	1966 %	1971 %
Education	14.0	18.5	21.6
Defence	17.0	12.2	6.8
Health	7.8	9.9	13.8
Welfare	15.5	15.0	17.2
Transportation	13.5	12.8	10.3

SOURCE: OECD, 1976

TABLE 6.2

Share of GNP spent on public education,
Canada compared with seven other nations,
1961 and 1969

	1961 %	1969 %
Canada	4.6	8.3
Sweden	5.1	7.9
USSR	5.9*	7.3
United States	4.0†	6.3
United Kingdom	4.3	5.6
France	2.4*	4.5
Japan	4.1*	4.0
West Germany	2.9	3.6

SOURCE: OECD, 1976
* = 1960, † = 1959

TABLE 6.3
School enrolments as per cent of
population, Canada compared with
selected countries, 1970

Canada	30.9
United States	30.6
France	24.2
United Kingdom	19.8
Japan	21.2
USSR	25.8
Italy	20.5
West Germany	20.6
East Germany	23.2
India	14.2

SOURCE: OECD, 1976

TABLE 6.4
Regional distribution of expenditures on elementary and secondary education by
government source, Canada and Provinces, 1970/1 and 1979/80

	Federal		Provincial		Municipal	
	1971 %	1980 %	1971 %	1980 %	1971 %	1980 %
Canada	5.7	2.6	55.0	66.0	35.1	27.3
Newfoundland	5.2	0.4	84.5	89.0	0.8	2.1
PEI	13.7	6.4	63.6	92.7	22.1	–
Nova Scotia	7.4	1.8	53.6	79.4	36.5	17.0
New Brunswick	10.4	2.0	88.2	96.7	–	–
Quebec	6.5	1.4	57.6	79.7	38.5	14.3
Ontario	1.9	1.0	52.6	57.2	42.0	37.7
Manitoba	13.3	7.6	44.9	44.7	39.3	42.7
Saskatchewan	11.7	8.3	41.2	56.2	44.9	33.0
Alberta	4.8	3.9	55.8	62.1	36.3	30.4
British Columbia	5.0	3.5	55.2	56.6	34.6	36.1

SOURCE: SC 81-568

Figures

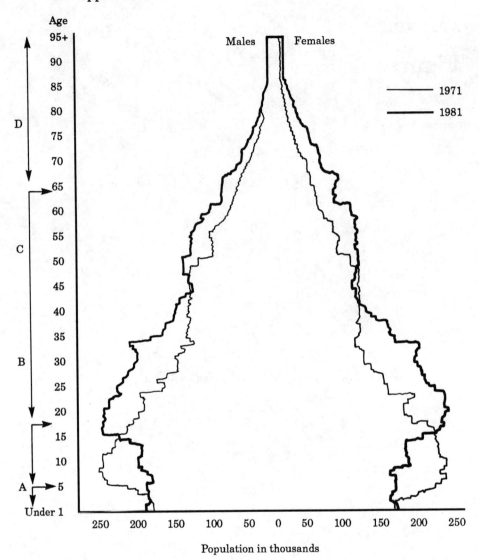

Figure 2.1
Age pyramid of the population of Canada, 1971 and 1981: A, pre-school
(ages 0–5); B, elementary and high school (ages 6–17); C, working age
(ages 18–64); D, retirement age population (ages 65–). SOURCE: 1971
Census of Canada, Catalogue 92-716, Table 14; 1981 Census of Canada,
Catalogue 92-901, Table 2

x 1,000

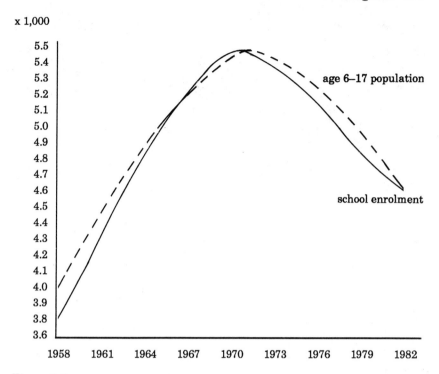

Figure 2.2
Elementary and secondary enrolment compared with population age 6–17.
SOURCE: SC 11-402, 81-210, 81-568, 81-569, 91-518

Enrolment x 1,000

Teachers x 1,000

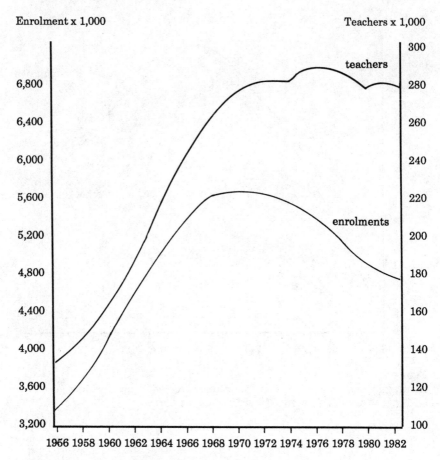

Figure 2.3
Change in teaching-force compared with change in school enrolment,
Canada, 1955–82. SOURCE: SC 81-229, 81-568, 81-569

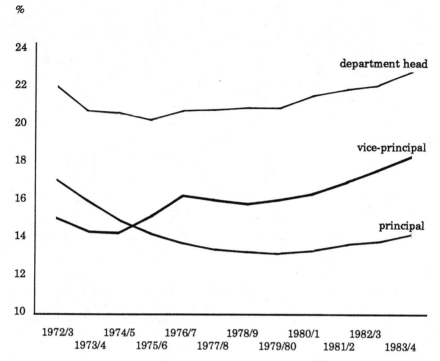

Figure 3.1
Percentage distribution of female educators in positions of added
responsibility, Canada, 1972/3 to 1983/4. SOURCE: SC 81-202 (83/4) Fig. 2,
p. 10

%

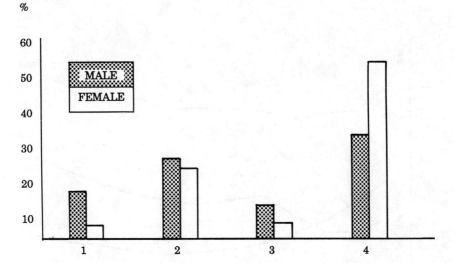

Figure 3.2
Percentage distribution of secondary teacher-education students by
father's occupational level, Ontario, 1959 (adapted from Watson, Quazi &
Poyntz, 1972): 1, unskilled & semi-skilled; 2, skilled; 3, semi-professional;
4, professional & executive

%

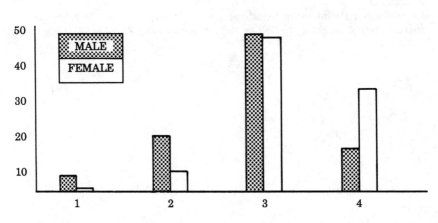

Figure 3.3
Percentage distribution of secondary teacher-education students by
father's occupational level, Ontario, 1964 (adapted from Watson, Quazi &
Poyntz, 1972): 1, unskilled & semi-skilled; 2, skilled; 3, semi-professional;
4, professional & executive

%

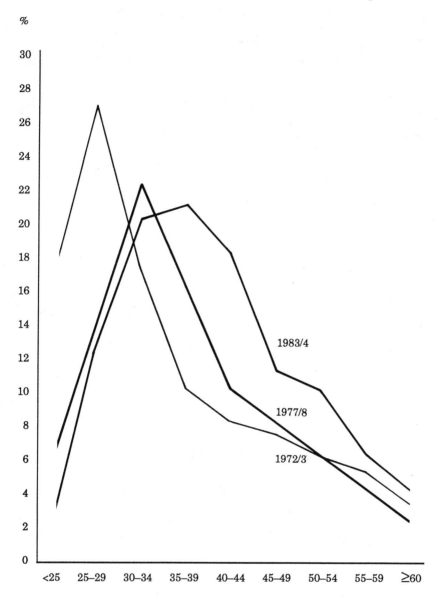

Figure 3.4
Age distribution of schoolteachers, Canada 1972/3, 1977/8, and 1983/4.
SOURCE: SC 81-202 (83/4), Fig. 1, p. 10

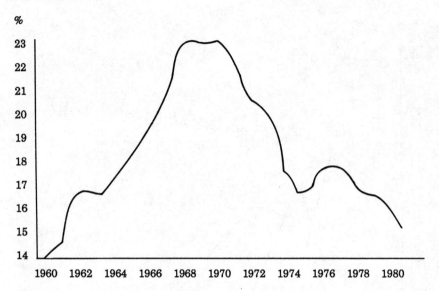

Figure 6.1
Government expenditures on education as per cent of total expenditures.
SOURCE: SC 81-560, 81-568

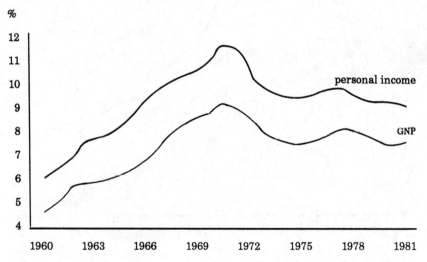

Figure 6.2
Total expenditures on education as per cent of personal income and GNP.
SOURCE: SC 81-560, 81-568

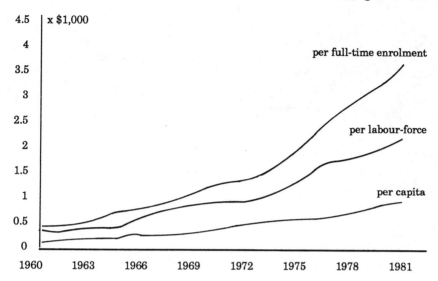

Figure 6.3
Total educational expenditures in relation to population variables.
SOURCE: SC 81-560, 81-568

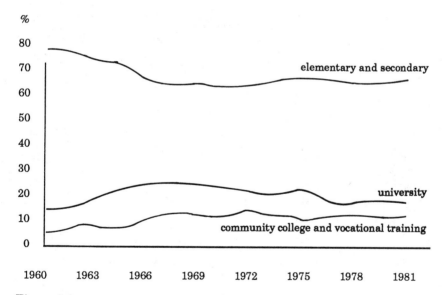

Figure 6.4
Distribution of educational expenditures by level. SOURCE: SC 81-560,
81-568

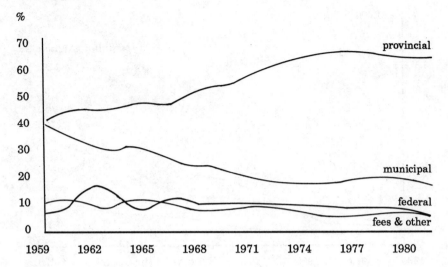

Figure 6.5
Distribution of educational expenditures by source. SOURCE: SC 81-560, 81-568

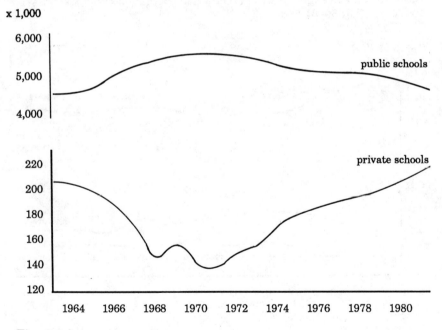

Figure 6.6
Public and private school enrolments, 1962/3 to 1981/2. SOURCE: SC 81–210

Data Bases Utilized in the Study

Canadian Class Structure Project. Carleton University, Sociology
Department, Ottawa
> Principal researchers: W. Clement, D. Forcese, J. Myles, and H.
> McRoberts. Part of an international data-gathering project.[1]
> The survey is a national, stratified sample of Canadians conducted in
> late 1982 and early 1983. Intensive interview scheduling required on
> average more than one hour of interviewing per respondent with up to
> five call-backs as required. This provided an exceptional depth of data
> not available from any other source. Special runs were utilized in this
> study.

Elementary-secondary School Enrollment Survey. Statistics Canada,
Ottawa
> Annual survey in co-operation with the provinces of all national and
> provincial public and private schools. Provides total population data on
> age, grade, gender distributions by region and school type. The basic
> data are published annually along with topical analysis in SC 81-210 and
> SC 81-220. Special runs were done for this study.

Highly Qualified Manpower Survey. Department of the Secretary of State
in collaboration with Statistics Canada
> A survey conducted in 1973 of a 138,000-person sample drawn from the
> 720,000 persons who reported in the 1971 census that they had a univer-

---

1 For a description of the international project, see Erik Olin Wright, et al, 'The
American Class Structure,' *American Sociological Review*, December 1982.

sity degree. Close to a 70 per cent return was obtained. The data collected covered educational qualifications, field of study, labour-force status, current earnings, and employment at different points in the respondent's career as well as the usual personal characteristic profiles. Two technical reports on the methodological characteristics and data analytical limitations of this data base are available from Statistics Canada. These are 'Methodology and Reliability Reports: Highly Qualified Manpower Post-Censal Survey (Ottawa 1974; revised 1975) and 'The Reliability and Validity of the Occupational Data in the 1973 HQMS' (Ottawa 1982). Special runs were done for this study.

Key Characteristics of Teachers in Public Elementary and Secondary Schools. Canadian Teachers' Federation, Ottawa
Combines Statistics Canada survey data with other regional data sources. These data, along with some analysis, are from time to time published by the federation (see Bibliography). Much of this is replication of what may be obtained from SC 81-202 publications, but is organized somewhat differently, reflecting the interests of the teacher-organization membership.

National Graduate Survey. Department of the Secretary of State and the Department of Employment and Immigration in collaboration with Statistics Canada, 1982
This stratified national survey sampled graduates of programs of over three months' duration in degree-granting universities, career/technical colleges, and recognized vocational training schools. The unit of analysis was the graduate (not the certification obtained). From the eligible population of 218,650 a sample of 49,150 was drawn. Both phone contacts and mail questionnaires were used. National response rates fell between 69 per cent and 81 per cent, depending on the educational program. A full discussion of methodology is available in unpublished mimeograph from the Special Surveys Branch of Statistics Canada: H. Hofman, 1982, 'National Graduates Survey: Survey Methodology Report' (Ottawa 1985). Special runs were done for this study.

Post Secondary Student Population Surveys. Dominion Bureau of Statistics (1968/9); Department of the Secretary of State in collaboration with Statistics Canada (1974/5 & 1982/3). Ottawa 1969, 1975, 1983
This data base consists of three successive national surveys:

- 1968/9: Surveys post-secondary students in programs of more than 26 weeks' duration. A stratified systematic sample yielded approximately 30,000 respondents.
- 1974/5: Similar to the first survey but with approximately 60,000 responses.
- 1982/3: Similar to the first two surveys with 60,000 responses. While the methods as well as the question frames differ somewhat from study to study, a high degree of compatibility between individual variables can be achieved through special runs. Methodological details for the 1968/9 survey are available from Statistics Canada, *Post-secondary Student Population Survey, 1968–69* (81-543); and for the 1974/5 survey from the Department of the Secretary of State publication *Some Characteristics of Post-secondary Students in Canada* (1976). A methodological review of the 1982/3 survey is not, at the time of this writing, yet available.

These surveys provide detailed data on post-secondary students' demographic, financial, study program, parental education, income, and occupational characteristics. Many of these data are unique and the (to date) three-cycle replication (along with some further compatibility with the Highly Qualified Manpower Study) provides opportunities for significant levels of longitudinal analysis. Special runs were done for this study.

Projections of Elementary and Secondary Enrollment and the Teaching Force in Canada. Canadian Teachers' Federation, Ottawa
Combines Statistics Canada population projections and enrolment survey data with other regional data sources to provide a somewhat more detailed data base. These data, along with some analysis, are from time to time published by the federation (see Bibliography).

Statistical Annex: Reviews of National Policies for Education. Paris
Comparative data base of public educational economic, demographic, and participation data in relation to overall population and national accounts for 53 countries.

Teacher Salary and Qualification Survey. Statistics Canada, Ottawa
Administered by the provincial ministries, these data are based on an annual survey of all public school educators. Statistics Canada then directly processes these data from Newfoundland, Prince Edward Island, New Brunswick, and the Territories. The remaining provinces forward

processed data to Statistics Canada, but in some cases with a delay. This causes some difficulties for early analysis, though historic data is maintained at a high level of accuracy. Basic frequencies and some ratios are published annually along with one or more items of topical analysis in SC 81-202. Special runs were done for this study.

References

Addington, R.J. 1965. 'Sampling Techniques for Administrative Decision-Making in Education.' MA thesis, University of Southern California

Allen, D.I., R. Hamilin, and G. Nixon. 1976. 'Need for Structure, Program Openness and Job Satisfaction among Teachers in Open Areas and Self-contained Classrooms.' *Alberta Journal of Educational Research* 22 (2): 149–53

Anisef, P. 1977. 'The Critical Juncture: An Exploration of Role Crystallization among Ontario Grade Twelve Students,' In Carlton, Colley, and MacKinnon (1977)

Anisef, P., N. Okihiro, and C. James. 1982. *Losers and Winners: The Pursuit of Equality and Social Justice in Higher Education.* Toronto: Butterworths

Arikado, M.S. 1977. 'Status Variables and Their Relationship to Team Teacher Satisfaction.' In Carlton, Colley, and MacKinnon (1977)

Armstrong, H. 1977. 'The Labour Force and State Workers in Canada.' In L. Panitch (ed), *The Canadian State: Political Economy and Political Power.* Toronto: University of Toronto Press

Bargen, P.F. 1961. *The Legal Status of the Canadian Public School Pupil.* Toronto: The Macmillan Co. of Canada

– 1972. 'Challenges to Educational Policy-Makers in the Decade Ahead.' In P.J. Cistone (ed), *School Boards and the Political Fact.* Toronto: The Ontario Institute for Studies in Education

Baron, G., and A. Tropp. 1961. 'Teachers in England and America.' In A.H. Halsey, J. Floud, and C.A. Anderson (eds), *Education, Economy, and Society.* New York: The Free Press of Glencoe

Battersby, D., and P. Ramsay. 1983. 'Professional Socialization of
  Teachers: Toward Improved Methodology.' *New Education* 5 (1): 77–86
Bayne, W.H. 1969. 'Local and Cosmopolitan Reference Group Saliency in
  the Calgary Public Schools.' MEd thesis, University of Calgary
Becker, H.S. 1953. 'The Teacher in the Authority System of the Public
  School.' *Journal of Educational Sociology* 27 (November): 137
Bell, D. 1977. 'On Meritocracy and Equality.' In J. Karabel and A.H.
  Halsey (eds), *Power and Ideology in Education*, 607–35. New York:
  Oxford University Press
Berg, I. 1970. *Education and Jobs: The Great Training Robbery.* New York:
  Praeger
Berkeley, H., C. Gaffield, and W.G. West. 1978. *Children's Rights: Legal
  and Educational Issues.* Toronto: The Ontario Institute for Studies in
  Education (Symposium Series 9)
Bezeau, L. 1980. *Public Education in Ontario is Excessively Capital
  Intensive.* Staff study, Ontario Institute for Studies in Education
Bledstein, B.J. 1978. *The Culture of Professionalism.* New York: Norton &
  Co.
Blishen, B.R. 1958. 'The Construction and Use of an Occupational Class
  Scale.' *Canadian Journal of Economics and Political Science* 24 (4):
  521–31
Bourne, P.T. 1970. 'Teacher Satisfaction and the Socio-Economic Status of
  School Attendance Areas.' MA thesis, University of Toronto
Branscombe, H.D.M. 1969. 'An Empirical Study of Teacher Professional-
  ism and Its Relationship to the Career Commitment and Local-Cos-
  mopolitan Orientations of Teachers in British Columbia Schools.' MA
  thesis, Simon Fraser University
Brant, C.S. 1977. 'Education for Canadian Eskimos.' In Carlton, Colley,
  and MacKinnon (1977)
Braverman, H. 1974. *Labor and Monopoly Capital.* New York: Monthly
  Review Press
Brimer, K. 1985. *A Content Analysis of Ontario Teacher Contracts: 1975 to
  1985.* Honours thesis, Trent University
Brown, D.J. 1980. *Financial Effects of Aid to Non-Public Schools: The
  British Columbia Experience.* Vancouver: Faculty of Education,
  University of British Columbia
Brown, L. 1979. 'Career Patterns of Male and Female Elementary Prin-
  cipals.' MA thesis. University of Calgary
Brown, W. 1969. *Educational Finance in Canada.* Ottawa: Canadian
  Teachers' Federation

Brubaker, H., and D.C. Patton. 1975. 'Selection and Retention in Teacher
Education: Does It Exist?' *The Teacher Educator* 10 (3): 2–8

Bruno, J.E., and I. Nelken. 1975. 'An Empirical Analysis on Propensity for
Teachers to Strike.' *Educational Administration Quarterly* 11 (2): 66–85

Butterick, J.A. 1977. *Educational Problems in Ontario and Some Policy
Options.* Occasional Paper 4. Toronto: Ontario Economic Council

Byrne, N., and J. Quarter, eds. 1972. *Must Schools Fail? The Growing
Debate in Canadian Education.* Toronto: McClelland and Stewart Ltd

Calam, J. 1977. 'Diversity and Despair in the Education of Teachers.' In
Stevenson and Wilson (1977)

Canadian Teachers' Federation. 1971a. *Collective Bargaining for Teachers.*
Ottawa: Canadian Teachers' Federation

– 1971b. *Merit Rating*

– 1973a. *New Goals, New Paths: The Search for a Rationale for the
Financing of Education in Canada*

– 1973b. *Teacher Autonomy and Teacher Decision Making*

– 1976. *Pre-Service Teacher Education in Canada*

– 1977. *Evaluation of Student Teachers*

– 1978a. *Decision Making In Education*

– 1978b. *Selection of Teachers and Student Teachers*

– 1978c. *Teacher Workload*

– 1980a. *Declining Enrolments*

– 1980b. *Pressure on Teacher Bargaining*

– 1980c. *Projections of Elementary and Secondary Enrolment and the
Teaching Force in Canada, 1979–80 to 1989–90*

– 1980d. *Public Expectations of Schools: The Professional Development
Response*

– 1981a. *Province-wide Assessment Programs: The Teachers' Response*

– 1981b. *Teacher and Administrator Evaluation*

– 1982. *Teacher Stress*

– 1983a. *Education for the 21st Century: Canadian Imperatives*

– 1983b. *Key Characteristics of Teachers in Public Elementary and Secondary Schools: 1972–73 to 1982–82*

– 1983c. *Teaching in Canada*

– 1984a. *Economic Recession and the Quality of Education*

– 1984b. *The Future of Collective Bargaining*

– 1984c. *Negotiated Surplus and Redundancy Provisions for Canadian
Teachers*

– 1984d. *Teacher Effectiveness Research.* Parts I & II

Carleton University. Department of Sociology. 1983. Canadian Class

Structure Project: Data Base. Data tapes, questionnaires, and code books available for analysis. Ottawa

Carlton, R.A., L.A. Colley, and N.J. MacKinnon, eds. 1977. *Education, Change, and Society: A Sociology of Canadian Education*. Toronto: Gage Educational Publications

Carr-Saunders, A.M., and P.A. Wilson. 1933. *The Professions*. London: Oxford University Press

Chation, A. 1977a. 'Attempts to Establish a National Bureau of Education, 1892–1926.' In A. Chation and N. McDonald (eds), *Canadian Schools and Canadian Identity*. Toronto: Gage Educational Publishing Ltd.

– 1977b. 'The National Council of Education: A Case Study of a Voluntary, Lay, Extra-Governmental Organization in the Inter-War Period.' In J.H.A. Wallin (ed), *The Politics of Canadian Education*, 19–26. Edmonton: Canadian Society for Studies in Education

Chapman, D.W. 1983. 'A Model of the Influences on Teacher Retention.' *Teacher Education* 34 (Sept.–Oct.): 43–9

Cicourel, A.V., and J.I. Kitsuse. 1963. *The Educational Decision-Makers*. New York: Bobbs-Merrill Co.

Cistone, P.J. 1972. 'The Politics of Education: Some Main Themes and Issues.' In P.J. Cistone (ed), *School Boards and the Political Fact*. Toronto: Ontario Institute for Studies in Education

Clark, S.C.T. 1970. 'Canadian Experience with Negotiations.' In *Negotiating for Professionalization*. Washington: National Education Association, National Commission on Teacher Education and Professional Standards

Clark, W., M.S. Devereaux, and Z. Zsigmond. 1979. *The Class of 2001: The School-Age Population – Trends and Implications, 1961 to 2001*. Statistics Canada and the Canadian Teachers' Federation

Clark, W., and Z. Zsigmond. 1981. *Job Market Reality for Postsecondary Graduates: Employment Outcomes by 1978, Two Years after Graduation*. Ottawa: Statistics Canada (81-572E). Ottawa: Ministry of Supply and Services

Cluett, E.J., and F. Buffett, eds. 1979. *Declining Enrolments: Implications for Teacher Supply and Demand*. St John's: Faculty of Education, Memorial University

Cole, Stephen. 1969. *The Unionization of Teachers: A Case Study of the UFT*. New York: Praeger

Coleman, J.S. 1966. *Equality of Educational Opportunity*. Washington: Office of Education, Department of Health, Education and Welfare

Coleman, P. 1977. 'Power Diffusion in Educational Governance: Redefining the Roles of Trustees and Administrators in Canadian Education.' In

J.H.A. Wallin (ed), *The Politics of Canadian Education*. Edmonton: Canadian Society for Studies in Education

— 1978. 'Shrinking Pains: Declining Enrolments, Fiscal Restraint, and Teacher Redundancy.' *McGill Journal of Education* 13 (1): 23–31

Colombotos, J. 1963. 'Sex Role and Professionalism: A Study of High School Teachers.' *The School Review* 71, (1): 27–40

Colucci, N.D., Jr. 1983. 'De-professionalizing Teaching: Now Enter the Courts.' *Contemporary Education* 54 (Spring): 212–15

Common, R.W. 1980. 'An Investigation of the Relationship between School Management Patterns and the Degree of Implementation of an Innovative Curriculum.' PhD dissertation, University of Ottawa

Connelly, F.M. 1975. 'Curriculum Decision Making by Teachers.' *Canadian Society for the Study of Education Bulletin* 2 (3)

Coombs, P.H. 1985. *The World Crisis in Education: The View from the Eighties*. New York: Oxford University Press

Cooper, W.M. 1966. 'An Investigation of Employer-Employee Relationships in Alberta School Jurisdictions.' MEd thesis, University of Alberta

Corman, L. 1979. *Declining Enrolments – Issues and Responses* (Bibliography No. 11). Toronto: The Ontario Institute for Studies in Education

Corwin, R.G. 1965. 'Militant Professionalism, Initiative and Compliance in Public Education.' *Sociology of Education* 38 (4): 310–31

— 1968. 'Teacher Militancy in the United States: Reflections on Its Sources and Prospects.' *Theory into Practice* 7 (April): 96–102

Cosine, M. 1970. 'An Empirical Study of the Relationships among Bureaucracy, Teacher Personality Needs and Teacher Satisfaction.' PhD dissertation, University of Ottawa

Crino, M.D., et al. 1983. 'Female Participation Rates and the Occupational Prestige of the Professions: Are They Inversely Related?' *Journal of Vocational Behavior* 22 (2): 243–55

Cunningham, J.B., and T.H. White (eds). 1984. *Quality of Working Life: Contemporary Cases*. Ottawa: Labour Canada, Ministry of Supply and Services

Cunningham, W. 1983. 'Teacher Burnout – Solutions for the 1980s: A Review of the Literature.' *The Urban Review* 15 (1): 37–51

Danylewycz, M., B. Light, and A. Prentice. 1983. 'The Evolution of the Sexual Division of Labour in Teaching: A Nineteenth-Century Ontario and Quebec Case Study.' *Social History* 16 (May): 81–109

Department of the Secretary of State. 1973. *A Directory of Federal Activities in the Field of Education 1972/73*. Ottawa: Department of the Secretary of State, Education Support Branch

Derber, C. 1983. 'Managing Professionals: Ideological Proletarianization and Post-Industrialization.' *Theory and Society* 12 (3): 309–41

Dickson, R.G.B. 1971. 'Consultation, Planning and Decision-Making Are Negotiable Items.' *ATA Magazine* 52 (Sept.–Oct.): 21–6

Dreeben, R. 1970. *The Nature of Teaching: Schools and the Work of Teachers*. Glenview, Ill.: Scott, Foresman & Co.

– 1977. 'The Contribution of Schooling to the Learning of Norms.' In J. Karabel and A.H. Halsey (eds), *Power and Ideology in Education*. New York: Oxford University Press. 544–9

Drummond, I. 1968. 'Labour Markets and Educational Planning.' In A. Kruger and N.M. Meltz (eds), *The Canadian Labour Market*. Toronto: Centre for Industrial Relations

Durkheim, e. 1957. *Professional Ethics and Civil Morals*. London: Routledge and Paul

– 1964. *The Division of Labor in Society*. New York: Free Press of Glencoe

Economic Council of Canada. 1964. *First Annual Review*. Ottawa

– 1965. *Second Annual Review*. Ottawa

Eddy, W.P. 1970. 'The Relationship of Role Orientation of Teachers to Organization of Schools.' *The Alberta Journal of Educational Research* 16 (1): 13–21

Educational Research Services, Inc. 1978. *Class Size: A Summary of Research*. Arlington, Va.: ERS Inc.

Edwards, C.E. 1965. 'School's Image in the Community: The Role of Home and School.' *Journal of Education (Nova Scotia)* 15: 18–21

Eichler, M. 1979. 'Sex-Role Attitudes of Male and Female Teachers in Ontario.' *Interchange* 10 (2): 2–14

Enns, F. 1963. *The Legal Status of the Canadian School Board*. Toronto: Macmillan Co. of Canada Ltd.

Enns, J., F. Dillon, and S. McDowell. 1975. *Implications of the employment of Auxiliary School Personnel*. Ottawa: Canadian Teachers' Federation

Epstein, C.F. 1970. 'Encountering the Male Establishment: Sex-Status Limits on Women's Careers in the Professions.' *American Journal of sociology* 75 (May): 965–82

Etzioni, A., ed. 1969. *The Semi-Professionals and Their Organization*. New York: Free Press

Evans, M.D., and E.O. Laumann. 1983. 'Professional Commitment: Myth and Reality?' *Research in Social Stratification and Mobility* 2: 3–40

Fagan, M.J., and W. Clarke, 1979. 'Predictors of Employment for the 1977–78 Teacher Education Graduating Class.' In Cluett and Buffett (1979)

Falk, W.W., et al. 1982. 'Professionalism and Conflict in a Bureaucratic Setting: The Case of a Teachers' Strike.' *Social Problems* 29 (5): 551–60

Farquhar, R.H., and I.E. Housego. 1988. *Canadian and Comparative Educational Administration*. Vancouver: Centre for Continuing Education, The University of British Columbia

Feistritzer, C.E. 1983. *The Condition of Teaching: A State by State Analysis*. Princeton, NJ: The Carnegie Foundation for the Advancement of Teaching

Ference, T.P., F.H. Goldner, and R.R. Ritti. 1973. 'Priests and Church: The Professionalization of an Organization.' In Freidson (1973a)

Fleming, W.G. 1971a. *Ontario's Educative Society / I: The Expansion of the Education System*. Toronto: University of Toronto Press

– 1971b. *Ontario's Educative Society / II: The Administrative Structure*. Toronto: University of Toronto Press

– 1971c. *Ontario's Educative Society / III: Schools, Pupils, and Teachers*. Toronto: University of Toronto Press

Floud, J., and W. Scott. 1961. 'Recruitment to Teaching in England and Wales.' In A.H. Halsey, J. Floud, and C.A. Anderson (eds), *Education, Economy, and Society*. New York: The Free Press of Glencoe

Flower, G.E. 1964. *How Big Is Too Big? Problems of Organizational Size in Local School Systems*. Toronto: W.J. Gage & Co.

Fluxgold, H. 1972. *Federal Support for Secondary Education and Its Effect on Ontario: 1900–1972*. Ottawa: Canadian Teachers' Federation

Folger, J.K., and C.B. Nam. 1964. 'Trends in Education in Relation to the Occupational Structure.' *Sociology of Education* 38 (Fall): 19–33

Fox, W.S., and M.H. Wince. 1976. 'Structure and Determination of Occupational Militancy among Public School Teachers.' *Industrial and Labour Relations Review* 23: 380–95

Francoeur, K. 1963. 'Factors of Satisfaction and Dissatisfaction in the Teaching Profession.' MEd thesis, University of Alberta

Fraser, G.S. 1970. 'Organizational Properties and Teacher Reactions.' *comparative Education Review* 14: 20–9

Freidson, E., ed. 1971. *The Professions and Their Prospects*. Beverly Hills: Sage Publications

– 1973. 'Professions and the Occupational Principle.' In E. Friedson (ed), *The Professions and Their Prospects*. 2d ed. Beverly Hills: Sage Publications

– 1983. 'The Reorganization of the Professions by Regulation.' *Law and Human Behavior* 7 (2–3): 279–90

Friedmann, G. 1955. *Industrial Sociology*. New York: Free Press

Fris, J. 1972. 'Professional Role Aspirations and Achievements among Ontario Secondary School Teachers.' MA thesis, University of Toronto
– 1976. 'Professionalisation and Militancy among Ontario Secondary School Teachers.' PhD dissertation, University of Toronto
Fullan, M., G. Eastabrook, and J. Biss. 1977. 'Action Research in the School: Involving Students and Teachers in Classroom Change.' In Carlton, Colley, and MacKinnon (1977)
Fullerton, S., and W.J. Brown. 1980. *Negotiated Surplus and Redundancy Provisions for Canadian Teachers*. Ottawa: Canadian Teachers' Federation
Gaffield, C., and W.G. West. 1978. 'Children's Rights in the Canadian Context.' In Berkeley, Gaffield, and West (1978)
Gajewsky, S. 1973. *Class Size: Review of the Literature and Selected Annotated Bibliography* (Reports in Education no. 2). Montreal: Faculty of Education, McGill University
Gerarda, Sr M., and R.R. O'Reilly. 1978. 'Acceptance of Parent Volunteers and Teacher Professionalism.' *Canadian Journal of Education* 3 (2): 67–74
Giles, T.E. 1974. *Educational Administration in Canada*. Calgary: Detselig Enterprises
Gill, N. 1967. 'The Relationship between the Size of Urban School Systems and Certain Characteristics of Their Administrative Staff.' MEd thesis, University of Alberta
Gills, J.C., Jr. 1969. 'Performance Contracting for Public Schools.' *Educational Technology*, May: 17–20
Globe and Mail, 7 May 1985. '9 school trustees fired by B.C. government in spending cutbacks.' Toronto
– 8 May 1985. 'Teachers support Vancouver board.' Toronto
Goffman, E. 1961. *Asylums*. Garden City: Anchor Books
Golden, M. 1974. 'York: The Winter of Discontent.' *Community Schools* 4 (March): 6–11
Goldenberg, S.B. 1968. *Professional Workers and Collective Bargaining: An Analysis of the Problems Which Professional Workers and Their Employers Face When They Adopt a Collective Bargaining Relationship*. Ottawa: Task Force on Labour Relations
Goode, W. 1966. '"Professions" and "Non-professions."' In Vollmer and Mills (1974)
Goodman, P. 1964. *Compulsory Mis-Education*. New York: Horizon Press
Gosin, M. 1970. 'An Empirical Study of the Relationship among Bureaucracy, Teacher Personality Needs, and Teacher Satisfaction.' Phd dissertation, University of Ottawa

Gosin, M., and M.V. Keith. 1970. 'Bureaucracy, Teacher Personality Needs and Teacher Satisfaction.' *The Canadian Administrator* 10 (1): 1–5

Gossage, C. 1977. *A Question of Privilege: Canada's Independent Schools.* Toronto: Peter Martin Associates

Grant, G. 1969. *Technology and Empire: Perspectives on North America.* Toronto: House of Anansi

Greene, M., and V. Dravland. 1981. 'Relationship between Success in an Education Program and Success in the Teaching Profession.' *Canadian Journal of Education* 6 (1): 5–17

Greenwood, E. 1957. 'Attributes of a Profession.' In *Social Work* 2 (3): 3–4

Greffen, G. 1969. 'Local-Cosmopolitan Orientation of Teachers and Their Compliance Tendencies.' MEd thesis, University of Calgary

Gregory, A. 1976. 'The Effects of Student Teaching on the Professional Self-concept of Student Teachers: A Study of Teachers in the Professional Development Program, Simon Fraser University.' PhD dissertation, Simon Fraser University

Gregory, A., and D.I. Allen. 1978. 'Some Effects of the Practicum on the Professional Self-Concept of Student Teachers.' *Canadian Journal of Education* 3 (2): 53–65

Hall, E.M., and L.A. Dennis (co-chairmen). 1968. *Living and Learning: The Report of the Provincial Committee on Aims and Objectives of Education in the Schools of Ontario.* Toronto: Ontario Department of Education

Hall, O. 1946. 'The Informal Organization of the Medical Profession.' *Canadian Journal of Economics and Political Science* 22: 30–44

– 1948. 'The Stages of a Medical Career.' *American Journal of Sociology* 53 (5): 327–36

– 1961. 'Some Pitfalls of Bigness.' In J.P. Kidd and C. Williams (eds), *New Developments in Society.* Ottawa: Canadian Conference on Education

– 1977. 'The Study of Education as a Complex Organization.' In Carlton, Colley, and MacKinnon (1977)

Hall, R.H. 1968. 'Professionalization and Bureaucratization.' *American Sociological Review* 33 (February): 92–104

– 1969. *Occupations and the Social Structure.* Englewood Cliffs, NJ: Prentice-Hall

– 1983. 'Theoretical Trends in the Sociology of Occupations.' *The Sociological Quarterly* 24 (1): 5–23

Hallingshead, A.B. 1949. *Elmtown's Youth.* New York: Wiley & Sons

Hamachek, D. 1969. 'Characteristics of Good Teachers and Implications for Teacher Education.' *Phi Delta Kappan* 50 (6)

Hamm-Brucher, H. 1981. 'Canadian Education: A View from Abroad.' In Wilson (1981)

Hare, W.F. 1975. 'The Disappearing Teacher.' In M.J.B. Jackson (ed), *Schools, Freedom and Authority: Seven Philosophical Essays.* St John's: Faculty of Education, Memorial University

Harp, J., and G. Betcherman. 1980. 'Contradictory Class Locations and Class Action: The Case of School Teachers' Organizations in Ontario and Quebec.' *Canadian Journal of sociology* 5 (2): 145–62

Harvey, E. 1974. *Educational Systems and the Labour Market.* Don Mills: Longman Canada

Haug, M.R., and M.B. Sussman, 1969. 'Professional Autonomy and the Revolt of the Client.' *Social Problems* 17 (2): 153–60

– 1973. 'Professionalization and Unionism: A Jurisdictional Dispute?' In Freidson (1973)

Havighurst, R.J. 1958. 'Education and Social Mobility in Four Societies.' *International Review of Education* 4 (2)

Havighurst, R.J., and D.U. Levine. 1979. *Society and Education,* 5th ed. Boston: Allyn and Bacon, Inc.

Hawkes, P.E. 1969. 'Collective Bargaining by Canadian Teachers: An Analysis of the Issues.' MEd thesis, University of New Brunswick

Hearn, J. 1982. 'Notes on Patriarchy, Professionalization and the Semi-Professions.' *Sociology* 16 (2): 184–202

Hellriegel, D., W. French, and R. Peterson. 1970. 'Collective Negotiations and Teachers: A Behavioral Analysis.' *Industrial and Labour Relations Review* 23: 380–95

Henchey, N. 1977. 'Pressures for Professional Autonomy and Public Controls.' In Stevenson and Wilson (1977)

– 1981. 'Alternatives to Decay: Prospects for the Teaching Profession in the Eighties.' In Wilson (1981)

Hennessy, P.H. 1975. *Teacher Militancy: A Comparative Study of Ontario, Quebec and New York Teachers.* Ottawa: Canadian Teachers' Federation

Hewitson, M.T. 1975. 'The Professional Satisfaction of Beginning Teachers.' PhD dissertation, University of Alberta

Hiebert, B., and I. Farber. 1984. 'Teacher Stress: A Literature Survey with a Few Surprises.' *Canadian Journal of Education* 9 (Winter): 14–27

Hodge, R.W., P.M. Siegel, and P.H. Rossie. 1964. 'Occupational Prestige in the United States, 1925–73.' *American Journal of sociology* 70: 286–302

Hodgetts, A.b. 1968. *What Culture? What Heritage? A Study of Civic Education in Canada.* Toronto: The Ontario Institute for Studies in Education

Hodgson, E. 1972. 'Community Schools.' In Cistone (1972)

Hoffman, N. 1981. *Womens' "True" Profession*. New York: McGraw-Hill

Holdaway, E.A. 1970. 'What Topics Are Discussed at School Board Meetings?' *School Progress* 39 (4)

– 1978. *Satisfaction of Teachers in Alberta with Their Working Conditions*. Edmonton: The University of Alberta

Holland, J. 1973. 'A Reappearance of National and Provincial Educational Policy Styles.' *Canadian and International Education* 2 (1): 47–65

Hollingshead, A.B. 1949. *Elmtown's Youth*. New York: Wiley and Sons

Housego, I.E. 1972. 'Pluralist Politics and Educational Decision-Making.' In Cistone (1972)

Hoyle, E. 1969. 'Organization Theory and Educational Administration.' In G. Baron and W. Taylor (eds), *Educational Administration and the Social Sciences*. London: Athlone Press

– 1980. 'Professionalization and Deprofessionalization in Education.' In E. Hoyle and J. Megarry (eds), *World Year Book of Education*. London: Cogan Page

Hughes, E.c. 1960. 'The Professions and Society.' *Canadian Journal of Economics and Political Science* 26 (1): 54–61

Hull, Jeremy. 1987. *An Overview of the Educational Characteristics of Registered Indians in Canada*. Ottawa: Indian and Northern Affairs Canada

Husby, P.J. 1979. *Public Funding and Control of Private Schools: Canadian-U.S. Comparisons*. Winnipeg: Faculty of Education, University of Manitoba

Husen, T. 1974. 'Standard of the Elite in Selective and Comprehensive Systems.' In *Talent, Equality and Meritocracy*. The Hague: Martinus Nijhoff

Illich, I. 1970. *Deschooling Society*. New York: Harper & Row

– ed. 1977. *Disabling Professions*. London: Marion Boyars

Inkeles, A., and P. Rossi. 1956. 'National Comparisons of Occupational Prestige.' *The American Journal of Sociology* 61: 329–39

Isherwood, G.B., et al. 1978. 'Quebec Educational Labour-Management Relations: A Case of Power Centralization.' *McGill Journal of Education* 13 (1): 32–48

Jackson, J., ed. 1970. *Professions, and Professionalization*. Cambridge: Cambridge University Press

Jackson, R.W.B. 1977a. *Canada 1977: A Demographic Mirage?, or the Myth of the 'Echo' of the Baby Boom*. Halifax: Atlantic Institute of Education

– 1977b. *Implications for Education of Recent Trends in Live Births and International and Interprovincial Migration of Children*. Toronto: The Canadian Education Association

– 1978. *The Challenge of Declining Enrolments: Critical Emerging Problems and Recommendations for Immediate Action*. Toronto: Commission on Declining School Enrolments in Ontario

Jencks, C. 1970. 'Education Vouchers.' *The New Republic*. 163 (4 July): 19–21

Jessup, D.K. 1978. 'Teacher Unionization: A Reassessment of Rank and File Motivations.' *Sociology of Education* 51: 44–5

Johnson, B. 1971. 'An Investigation of Teachers' Salary and Working Conditions in Selected School Jurisdictions in Alberta 1960–1969.' PhD dissertation, University of Alberta

Johnson, F.H. 1968. *A Brief History of Canadian Education*. Toronto: McGraw-Hill Co. of Canada Ltd.

Johnson, T.J. 1972. *Professions and Power*. London: Macmillan

Jones, F.E. 1963. 'The Social Origins of High School Teachers in a Canadian City.' *Canadian Journal of Economics and Political Science* 29 (4): 529–35

Jones, P.A. 1980. 'Professionalization, Bureaucratization and Conflict in Secondary School counsellors.' MEd thesis, University of Manitoba

Katz, J. 1974. *Education in Canada*. Vancouver: Douglas, David and Charles

King, A.J.C., and R.A. Ripton. 1970. 'Teachers and Students: A Preliminary Analysis of Collective Reciprocity.' *The Canadian Review of Sociology and Anthropology* 7 (1): 35–48

King, L.R., and P.H. Malaanson. 1972. 'Knowledge and Politics: Some Experiences from the 1960s.' *Public Policy* 20 (1)

Kleingartner, A., and M. Liang Bickner. 1977. 'Scope of Bargaining and Participation in Decision Making by Professionals.' In F. Hinman (ed), *Professional Workers and Collective Bargaining*. Los Angeles: Institute of Industrial Relations, University of California

Knoop, R. 1980. *An Inventory of Competency Statements for Teachers, Principals and Superintendents*. Toronto: Ontario Ministry of Education

Koerner, J.D. 1963. *The Mis-education of American Teachers*. New York: Houghton Mifflin

Kornhauser, W. 1962. *Scientists in Industry: Conflict and Accommodation*. Los Angeles: University of California Press

Kratzmann, A. 1974. 'Trustee Responsibility and Teacher Power – Understanding the Basic Issues.' Toronto: Ontario Institute for Study in Education

Lam, J. 1982. 'Teacher Professional Profile – A Personal and Contextual Analysis.' *Alberta Journal of Educational Research* 28 (2): 122–34

– 1983. 'Attitudes towards Professionalism in Today's Teaching Force.' *Education Canada* 23 (1): 27–31

Lamontagne, Jacques. 1977. 'The Rise and Fall of Classical Education in Quebec: A Systemic Analysis.' In Carlton, Colley, and MacKinnon (1977)

Langford, G. 1978. *Teaching as a Profession*. Manchester: Manchester University Press

LaNoue, G.R. 1971. 'Vouchers: The End of Public Education?' *Teacher's College Record* 73 (December): 304–19

Larson, M.S. 1977. *The Rise of Professionalism*. Berkeley: University of California Press

Lasley, T.J., and C.M. Galloway. 1983. 'Achieving Professional Status: A Problem in What Teachers Believe.' *Clearing House* 57 (September): 5–8

Laxer, G., R.E. Traub, and K. Wayne. 1974. *Student Social and Achievement Patterns as Related to Secondary School Organizational Structures*. Toronto: Ontario Institute for Studies in Education

Lessinger, L.M. 1969. 'Accountability for Results: A Basic Challenge for America's Schools.' *American Education* 5 (June–July): 2–4

Liberman, J.K. 1970. *The Tyranny of the Experts*. New York: Walker and Co.

Linderfeld, F. 1961. *Teacher Turnover in Public Elementary and Secondary Schools, 1959–60*. Washington, DC: Office of Education, Department of Health, Education, and Welfare

Lipset, S.M., and M.A. Schwartz. 1966. 'The Politics of Professionals.' In Vollmer and Mills (1966)

Livingston, D.W. 1979. *Public Attitudes toward Education in Ontario 1978*. Toronto: The Ontario Institute for Studies in Education

– 1981. 'Public Priorities for Education in Capitalistic Crisis.' In Wilson (1981)

Livingston, D.W., and D.J. Hart. 1980. *Public Attitudes toward Education in Ontario 1979*. Toronto: The Ontario Institute for Studies in Education

Lockhart, A. 1971. 'Graduate Unemployment and the Myth of Human Capital.' In D.I. Davies and K. Herman (eds), *Social Space: Canadian Perspectives*. Toronto: New Press

– 1975. 'Future Failure: The Unanticipated Consequences of Educational Planning.' In R. Pike and E. Zureik (eds), *Socialization and Values in Canadian Society*. Toronto: McClelland and Stewart

– 1977. 'Educational Policy Development in Canada: A Critique of the Past and a Case for the Future.' In Carlton, Colley and MacKinnon (1977)

– 1979. 'Educational Opportunities and Economic Opportunities – The "New" Liberal Equality Syndrome.' In J.A. Fry (ed), *Economy, Class and Social Reality: Issues in Contemporary Canadian Society*, 224–377. Toronto: Butterworths

Loosemore, J., and R.A. Carlton. 1977. 'The Student-Teacher: A Dramaturgic Approach to Role-Learning.' In Carlton, Colley, and MacKinnon (1977)

Lortie, D. 1959. 'Laymen to Lawmen: Law School, Careers, and Professional Socialization.' *Harvard Educational Review* 29 (4): 363–7

– 1975. *School Teacher: A Sociological Study*. Chicago: University of Chicago Press

Lucas, B.G., and C.S. Lusthaus. 1977. 'Do Schools Reach Out to Parents?' *McGill Journal of Education* 12 (2): 253–60

Lutz, F.W. 1972. 'Teacher Organizations and Teacher Power.' In Cistone (1972)

Macdonald, J. 1970. *The Discernible Teacher*. Ottawa: Canadian Teachers' Federation

Machlup, F. 1962. *The Production and Distribution of Knowledge in the United States*. Princeton: Princeton University Press

MacIver, D.A. 1973. 'The Limits of Community Schools.' In Myers (1973)

MacIver, R. 1955. 'The Social Significance of Professional Ethics.' *The Annals of the American Academy of Political and Social Science* 297 (January): 118–24

Mackie, M. 1972. 'School Teachers: The Popular Image.' *Alberta Journal of Educational Research* 18 (4): 267–76

MacKinnon, Frank. 1960. *The Politics of Education*. Toronto: University of Toronto Press

MacLeod, C.R. 1973. 'Anatomy of a Teachers' Strike.' *Education Canada* 13 (December): 47–50

Marcotte, W.A. 1984. *Teachers' Collective Agreements*. Ottawa: Council of Ministers of Education, Canada

Marcus, P.M. 1973. 'Schoolteachers and Militant Conservatism.' In Freidson (1971)

Marien, M. 1971. 'Beyond Credentialism: The Future of Social Selection.' *Social Policy* 2 (3): 14–21

Martell, G. 1974. *The Politics of the Canadian Public School*. Toronto: James Lewis & Samuel

Martin, W.B. 1976. *The Negotiated Order of the School*. Toronto: Macmillan Co. of Canada Ltd.

– 1979. 'Teachers' Perceptions of Their Interaction Tactics.' *Education* 99(3): 236–9

Martin, W.B., and Allan J. Macdonell. 1982. *Canadian Education: A Sociological Analysis*. 2nd ed. Scarborough, Ont.: Prentice-Hall Canada Inc.

Maxwell, M.P., and J.D. Maxwell. 1971. 'Boarding School: Social Control, Space and Identity.' In D.I. Davies and K. IIerman (eds), *Social Space: Canadian Perspectives*. Toronto: New Press

Mayer, M. 1969. *The Teacher Strike: New York, 1968*. New York: Harper & Row

Millerson, G. 1964. *The Qualifying Association: A Study in Professionalization*. London: Routledge and Kegan Paul

Montagna, P.D. 1973. 'The Public Accounting Profession: Organization, Ideology and Social Power.' In Freidson (1973a)

Moore, W.E. 1970. *The Professions: Roles and Rules*. New York: Russell Sale Foundation

Muendel-Atherstone, B. 1980. *A Personality Profile of Students Who Are Successful in Student Teaching and in Teaching*. Lethbridge: Faculty of Education, University of Lethbridge

Muir, J.D. 1970. 'Canadian School Teacher Salaries: Impact of Collective Bargaining and Other Factors.' PhD dissertation, Cornell University

Murray, J. 1979. *Public Opinions and Attitudes toward Education: 654 Personal Interviews*. Toronto: The Board of Education for the Borough of York

Myers, D., ed. 1973. *The Failure of Educational Reform in Canada*. Toronto: McClelland and Stewart Ltd.

– 1974. 'Teacher Militancy: Trend for the 70s?' *Quill and Quire* 40 (October): 14, 16, 18

Myhre, A. 1971. 'The Politics of Educational Change at the Local Level.' In T.J. Sawchuk and R.G. McIntosh (eds), *Council on School Administration*. Edmonton: Alberta Teachers' Association

Nash, P. 1962. 'The Future of Educational Research in Canada.' *Canadian Education and Research Digest*, September: 161–72

Nash, R.J., and R.M. Agne. 1972. 'The Ethos of Accountability – A Critique.' *Teachers College Record* 73 (February): 357–69

Nelson, F. 1973. 'Community Schools in Toronto: A Sign of Hope.' In Myers (1973)

Newberry, J.M. 1979. 'The Beginning Teacher's Search for Assistance from Colleagues.' *Canadian Journal of Education* 4 (1): 17–27

Nordstrom, C., E.Z. Friedenberg, and H.A. Gold. 1967. *Society's Children: A Study of Ressentiment in the Secondary School*. New York: Random House

North, C., and P. Hatt. 1949. 'Jobs and Occupations: A Popular Evaluation.' In L. Wilson and W.A. Kolb (eds), *Sociological Analysis*. New York: Harcourt Brace Jovanovich

Nutter, N. 1983. 'Why Students Drop Out of Teacher Education.' *Action Teacher Education* 5 (Spring–Summer): 25–32

l'Office des professions du Québec. 1976. *The Evaluation of Professionalism in Quebec*. Quebec: Office des professions

Office of Education. 1967. *Teacher Turnover, 1959–60*. Washington DC: Office of Education, Department of Health, Education, and Welfare

Ontario Teachers' Federation Commission. 1968. 'Patterns for Professionalism.' Report to the Board of Governors of the Ontario Teachers' Federation

Oppenheimer, M. 1970. 'The Proletarianization of the Professional.' *Sociological Review* 20 (Summer)

Organization for Economic Co-operation and Development. 1976. *Reviews of National Policies for Education: Canada*. Paris: OECD

Paci, M. 1977. 'Education and the Capitalist Labor Market.' In J. Karabel and A.H. Halsey (eds), *Power and Ideology in Education*, 340–55. New York: Oxford University Press

Page, J.A. 1983. 'Preservice and Inservice Teachers Hold Differing Perceptions of Teaching.' *Phi Delta Kappan* 64 (May): 662–3

Pallesen, L.C. 1970. 'Teacher Satisfaction with a Computer Assisted Placement in the Secondary Schools of a Large Urban System.' PhD dissertation, University of Calgary

Palmatier, L.L. 1969. 'Teacher Power and Professionalism in California.' PhD dissertation, University of California, Berkeley

Parry, R.S. 1970. 'Teacher Staff Turnover and Organization Structure.' PhD dissertation, University of Calgary

Parsons, T. 1939. 'The Professions and Social Structure.' *Social Forces* 17 (4): 457–67

Paton, J.M. 1962. *The Role of Teachers' Organizations in Canadian Education*. Toronto: W.J. Gage

– 1970. 'Movements toward Teacher Autonomy in Canada.' *Phi Delta Kappan* 52 (September): 45–9

Pavalko, R.M. 1970. 'Recruitment to Teaching: Patterns of Selection and Retention.' *Sociology of Education* 43 (Summer): 340–53

– 1971. *The Sociology of Occupations and Professions*. Ithaca, Ill.: F.E. Peacock Publishers

Pelton, A.J. 1977. 'The Ambiguous Role of the Teacher-Counsellor in Secondary Schools.' In Carlton, Colley, and MacKinnon (1977)

Picot, W.G. 1983. *University Graduates and Jobs: Changes during the 1970s*. Ottawa: Statistics Canada

Pidgeon, D. 1974. 'Class Size as a Factor in Pupil Performance.' In Organisation for Economic Co-operation and Development, *New Patterns of Teacher Education and Tasks*. Paris: OECD

Pierce, H.L. 1974. 'Reference Groups and Significant Others of Student Teachers.' *Alberta Journal of Educational Research* 20 (2): 170–7

Pike, R.M. 1981. 'Contemporary Directions and Issues in Education: A Sociologist's View of the Last Twenty Years.' In Wilson (1981)

Pineo, P.C., and J. Porter. 1967. 'Occupational Prestige in Canada.' *The Canadian Review of Sociology and Anthropology* 4: 24–40

Ponak, A. 1981. 'Unionized Professionals and the Scope of Bargaining.' *Industrial and Labour Relations Review* 34 (3): 396–407

Porter, John. 1965. *The Vertical Mosaic*. Toronto: University of Toronto Press

Prentice, A. 1978. *The School Promoters*. Toronto: McClelland and Stewart

Quarter, J. 1972. 'The Teacher's Role in the Classroom: The Primary Source of Teacher Frustration and Discontent.' In Byrne and Quarter (1972)

Radecki, H., and S. Evans. 1980. *The Teacher Strike Study: Sudbury, Ontario*. Toronto: Ontario Ministry of Education

Ratsoy, E.W. 1966. 'Professional Attitudes of Prospective Teachers.' *The Canadian Administrator* 5 (8): 31–4

– 1975. 'Professionalism in Education: The Optimistic Approach.' In *Selected Readings in Educational Administration*. Edmonton: Department of Educational Administration, University of Alberta

Regan, G. 1977. 'Socialization Outcomes and Processes in Canadian Schooling.' In Carlton, Colley, and MacKinnon (1977)

Richards, C.R. 1978. 'Non-Public Schools Experience Mini-Boom.' *School Business Affairs* 44 (1): 17–18

Rinehart, J.W. 1975. *The Tyranny of Work*. Don Mills: Longman Canada

Romaniuc, A. 1984. *Current Demographic Analysis – Fertility in Canada: From Baby-Boom to Baby-Bust*. Ottawa: Statistics Canada

Rosenthal, R., and L. Jacobson. 1966. 'Teachers' Expectancies: Determinants of Pupils' IQ Gains.' *Psychology Reports* 19: 115–18

– 1968. *Pygmalion in the Classroom*. New York: Holt, Rinehart, and Winston

Roth, R. 1983. 'The Status of the Profession: Selected Characteristics of Teacher Education and Teaching.' *Educator* 19 (2): 2–10

Ryan, D.W., and T.B. Greenfield. 1975. *The Class Size Question: Development of Research Studies Related to the Effects of Class Size, Pupil / Adult, and Pupil / Teacher Ratios*. Toronto: Ontario Ministry of Education

Ryans, D.G. 1960. *Characteristics of Teachers*. Washington, DC: American Council on Education

Schlechty, P.C., and V.S. Vance. 1981. 'Do Academically Able Teachers Leave Education? The North Carolina Case.' *Phi Delta Kappan* 63 (2): 106–12

Schmit, D.A. 1968. 'A Study of Teacher Satisfaction in Relation to Professional Orientation and Perceived Hierarchial Authority in the School.' MEd thesis, University of Alberta

Schon, D.A. 1983. *The Reflective Practitioner: How Professionals Think in Action*. New York: Basic Books

Schultz, T.W. 1961. 'Investment in Human Capital.' *American Economic Review* 51 (March): 1–17

Selby, J. 1977. 'The Myth of Local Control in Ontario Education.' In Carlton, Colley, and MacKinnon (1977)

Selinger, A.D. 1980. 'Attitudes of Ontario Secondary School Teachers toward Aspects of Professional Negotiations and Sanctions.' *Canadian Journal of Education* 5(3): 34–54

Selinger, A.D., and K. Goldhammer. 1972. 'The Roots of Teacher Militancy.' In Cistone (1972)

Seymour Wilson, V. 1977. 'Federal Perspectives on Education: Social, Political and Economic Policies.' In Stevenson and Wilson (1977)

Shack, S. 1973. *The Two-Thirds Minority*. Toronto: University of Toronto Press

Shaiken, H. 1977. 'Craftsman into Baby Sitter.' In Illich (1977)

Sheffield, E.F. 1970. 'The Post-War Surge in Post-Secondary Education: 1945–1969.' In Wilson, Stamp, and Audet (1970)

Sheldrick, K.D. 1974. 'The Erosion of Trustee Responsibility: Quebec: A Case Study.' Toronto: Ontario Institute for Studies in Education

Shepiro, H.S. 1983. 'Habermas, O'Connor and Wolfe, and the Crisis of the Welfare Capitalist State: Conservative Politics and the Roots of Educational Policy in the 1980s.' *Education Theory* 33 (Summer–Fall): 135–47

Simpkins, W.S., and D. Friesen. 1969. 'Teacher Participation in School Decision-Making.' *The Canadian Administrator* 8 (4): 13–16

– 1970. 'Discretionary Powers of Classroom Teachers.' *The Canadian Administrator* 9 (8): 35–8

Slocum, W.L. 1966. *Occupational Careers*. Chicago: Aldine Publishing Co.

Small, D.P. 1970. 'Teaching and Commitment: A Study of Newfoundland Teachers.' MA thesis, Memorial University of Newfoundland

Spady, W.G. 1977. 'Power, Authority and Empathy in Schooling.' In Carlton, Colley, and MacKinnon (1977)

Stabler, E. 1979. 'Self-Government and the Teaching Profession: A Comparison of Canada and Scotland.' *Canadian Journal of Education* 4 (2): 1–14

Stamp, R.M. 1970. 'Government and Education in Post-War Canada.' In Wilson, Stamp, and Audet (1970)

– 1975. *About Schools: What Every Canadian Parent Should Know*. Don Mills, Ont.: New Press

Statistics Canada. 1980. *A Comparative Analysis of Male/Female Staff in the Ontario Educational System, 1972 to 1979*. Ottawa: Affirmative Action Unit, Ministry of Supply and Services (hereafter MSS)

– 81-002 Monthly. *Education Statics* (formerly *Education Service Bulletin*). MSS

– 81-202 Annual. *Salaries and Qualifications of Teachers in Public Elementary and Secondary Schools*. MSS

– 81-208 Annual. *Financial Statistics of Education*. MSS

– 81-209 Annual. *Vocational and Technical Training*. MSS

– 81-210 Annual. *Elementary-Secondary School Enrolment*. MSS

– 81-214 Annual. *Statistics of Private Trade Schools and Business Colleges*. MSS

– 81-215 Annual. *Private Elementary and Secondary Schools*. MSS

– 81-216 Annual. *Interprovincial and International Migration of Children in Canada*. MSS

– 81-220 Annual. *Advance Statistics of Education*. MSS

– 81-222 Annual. *Enrolments in Community Colleges*. MSS

– 81-227 Annual. *Educational Staff in Community Colleges*. MSS

– 81-229 Occasional. *Education in Canada*. MSS

– 81-239 Annual. *Students in Public Trade Schools and Similar Institutions*. MSS

– 81-241 Annual. *Teachers in Universities*. MSS

– 81-250 Annual. *Elementary-Secondary Education: Financial Statistics*. MSS

– 81-251 Annual. *Educational Staff in Public Trade Schools and Similar Institutions*. MSS

– 81-254 Annual. *Educational Staff of Community Colleges and Vocational Schools*. MSS

168 References

– 81-258 Annual. *Salaries and Salary Scales of Full-time Teaching Staff at Canadian Universities.* MSS
– 81-259 Annual. *Postgraduation Plans of 1981 PHD Graduates.* MSS
– 81X-502 Occasional. *A Statistical Portrait of Canadian Higher Education from the 1960s to the 1980s: 1983 Edition.* MSS
– 81-547 1970/1. *Education in the Atlantic Provinces, 1970/71.* MSS
– 81-549 1970. *Education in Canada's Northland 1960/1970.* MSS
– 81-550 1971. *Century of Education in British Columbia: Statistical Perspectives, 1871–1971.* MSS
– 81-557 1972. *Education in the Western Provinces, 1971–72.* MSS
– 81-559 1972. *University Education Growth 1960/61 and 1971–72.* MSS
– 81-560 1969. *A Decade of Educational Finance, 1960–69.* MSS
– 81-561 1971. *Socio-Cultural Characteristics of Elementary and Secondary Students, 1971.* MSS
– 81-566 Occasional. *The Educational Profile of University Graduates.* MSS
– 81-568 Occasional. *Historical Compendium of Educational Statistics from Confederation to 1975.* MSS
– 81-571 Occasional. *1976 University and College Graduates: Doctoral Degree Recipients.* MSS
– 81-572 Occasional. *Job Market Reality for Postsecondary Graduates: Employment Outcome by 1978, Two Years after Graduation.* MSS
Stevenson, H.A., and J.D. Wilson. 1977. *Precepts, Policy and Process: Perspectives on Contemporary Canadian Education.* London, Ont.: Alexander, Blake Associates
Stinnett, T.M. 1969. *The Teacher Dropout.* Itasca, Ill.: F.E. Peacock Publishers, Inc.
Sykes, G. 1983a. 'Contradictions, Ironies and Promises Unfulfilled: A Contemporary Account of the Status of Teaching.' *Phi Delta Kappan* 65 (October): 87–93
– 1983b. 'Incentive-based Restructuring for the Teaching Profession.' *Education Digest* 49 (November): 10–13
Szasz, T.S. 1963. *Law, Liberty and Psychiatry.* New York: Macmillan
– 1974. *The Myth of Mental Illness.* New York: Harper and Row
Taylor, L. 1968. *Occupational Sociology.* New York: Oxford University Press
Taylor, W. 1965. 'The University Teacher of Education in England.' *Comparative Education* 1 (3): 193–201
Turner, R.H. 1964. *The Social Context of Ambition.* San Francisco: Chandler Publishing Co.

Valdes, A.L. 1982. *A Nationwide Survey of the Status of Teacher Competency Programs in the States*. Dover: Delaware Department of Public Instruction

Veevers, J.E. 1983. *Demographic Aspects of Vital Statistics: Fertility*. Ottawa: Statistics Canada

Villec, C. 1982. 'Education Students Rank Near Bottom.' *Wisconsin State Journal*, February

Villeme, M.G., and B.W. Hall. 1983. 'Higher Ability Education Graduates: Do They Enter and Stay in Teaching?' *Teacher Education* 19 (Winter): 11–15

Vollmer, H.M. 1966. 'Entrepreneurship and Professional Productivity among Research Scientists.' In H.M. Vollmer, and D.L. Mills, *Professionalization*, 276–82. Englewood Cliffs, NJ: Prentice-Hall

Wahlstrom, M.W. 1979. *Selection of Teacher Candidates: A Systematic Search for Criteria*. Toronto: Ontario Ministry of Education

Ward, B. 1974. *Women at Work*. Toronto: Canadian Women's Education Press

Warren, P.J. 1979a. *A Study of Unemployed Teachers*. St John's: Institute for Research and Development, Memorial University

– 1979b. 'Teacher Supply with Emphasis on Unemployment.' In Cluett and Buffett (1979)

Watson, C., S. Quazi, and J. Poyntz. 1972. *The Secondary Teacher*. Toronto: Ontario Institute for Studies in Education

Watts, D. 1984. 'Should Teaching Become a Come-and-Go Profession?' *Teacher Education* 35: 39–42

Weber, M. 1947. *The Theory of Social and Economic Organization* (ed. Talcott Parsons). New York: Oxford University Press

Weinzweig, P. 1977. 'Socialization in Canadian Private Schools: A Case Study.' In Carlton, Colley, and MacKinnon (1977)

Wilensky, H.L. 1964. 'The Professionalization of Everyone?' *American Journal of Sociology* 70 (September): 137–58

Wiles, D.K., and T.R. Williams. 1972. 'Political Realities of Trustee Effectiveness.' In Cistone (1972)

Williams, T., and M.J. Powell. 1980. 'Issues in Canadian Educational Administration.' In Farquhar and Housego (1980)

Wilson, J.D. 1977. 'From the Swinging Sixties to the Sobering Seventies.' In Stevenson and Wilson (1977)

– 1981. *Canadian Education in the 1980s*. Calgary: Detselig Enterprises Ltd.

Wilson, J.D., R.M. Stamp, and L.P. Audet, eds. 1970. *Canadian Education:*

A History. Scarborough, Ont.: Prentice-Hall of Canada

Wolf, B.T. 1984. 'The New Vocationalism and Teacher Education.' *Teacher Education* 35 (Jan.–Feb.): 21–5

Wuthnow, R., and W. Shrum. 1983. 'Knowledge Workers as a "New Class": Structural and Ideological Convergence among Professional-Technical Workers and Managers.' *Work and Occupations* 10 (4): 471–87

Young, D.G. 1979. 'A Futures Perspective of Control of Education in Canada.' *The Canadian Administrator* 28 (7): 1–5

Young, L.G. 1971. 'Is Collective Bargaining Compatible with Educational Objectives?' *Alberta School Trustee* 41 (April): 3–6

Young, Michael F.D. 1971. *Knowledge and Control: New Directions for the Sociology of Education*. London: Collier-MacMillan

Zsigmond, Z. 1975. 'Patterns of Demographic Change Affecting Education 1961–2001.' In *National Conference on Financing Education: The Challenge of Equity*. Conference proceedings, Quebec City, February 16–19. Ottawa: Canadian Teachers' Federation

– 1976. 'Population and Enrolment Trends: 1961–2001.' *Canadian Journal of Education* 1 (1): 19–38

Zsigmond, Z., et al. 1978. *Out of School – Into the Labour Force: Trends and Prospects for Enrolment, Schools Leavers and the Labour Force in Canada – the 1960s through the 1980s*. (Catalogue 81-570 Occasional). Ottawa: Statistics Canada

Zsigmond, S., and C. Wenaas. 1970. *Enrolment in Educational Institutions by Province, 1951/52 to 1980/81*. Ottawa: Economic Council of Canada

Index

174 Index

ment, 5; regulation, 5, 9, 11;
social contract, xi; socialization, 5, 47, 48, 49, 51, 55, 77;
unemployment, 8
Professionalism: bureaucratic
organization, 6; and humanism, 9, 11; ideology of, 7, 9;
independent practitioner, 14
Professionalization: power distribution, 7, 77, 89, 92; gender, 8;
legitimating ideology, 6, 7, 12;
monopoly, 8, 9; regulation, 11,
12
Public: accountability, xii, 11, 17,
34, 70, 97–101, 105, 107, 108,
110, 112; disenchantment, 10;
image, 28, 60, 83; interest,
110–14; policy, xii, 20, 23, 97–
105; relations, 9, 17, 85, 112;
security, 28; vulnerability, 28

Quality of work life, 59–60
Quintessential professions, xii

Reserve of title, 10
Role conflict, 73, 78, 111, 112
Ryerson, Egerton, 88

Salarization, 10
School administration, 16, 28
School Administration Act, 13
School trustees: competence, 14,
62, 100; community relations,
15; local control, 14
School-boards, 89, 93, 96; amal-
gamation of, 15. See also
School trustees
Schools: ideological environment,
51; operational environment,
51; physical plant, 15

Separate school system, 104–5
Silent firing, 25
Social: agent role, 6, 49, 59, 60,
73, 112; change, xi, 7, 66; conflict, 4, 5; contract, xi; control,
5, 74, 83, 112; distance, 101;
inequality, 59, 105, 106; integration, 5; mobility, 26, 35, 61,
81; norms, 27, 53; power, 92,
108; prejudice, 27; sorting
function, 54, 59, 83; stratification, 5; theories, xii; values, 27,
58
Socialization function, 83
Social-psychological factors, 61,
69
Socio-economic status (SES), 7,
27, 35, 55, 63, 78, 81–6
State: educational obligations of,
19, 98; functions of, 4; public
confrontation with, 93
Statistical data, levels of, xiii
Statistics Canada, xi, xv
Status: achieved, 82; ascription,
82; attainment, 81–6; deprivation, 84; inconsistency, 83, 111;
scales, 82
Strikebreakers, 94
Strikes, 85, 94
Students: achievement, 52, 59;
performance, 24; retention
rates, 21, 30; rights of, 109;
role ascription, 51
Student-teacher ratio, 22, 24, 34,
54
Subject specialization, 57, 58, 74
Superintendents, 71

Teachers: associations, 87–96,
109; attitudes, 48–54, 111;